FEDERAL RULES OF EVIDENCE HANDBOOK

with Common Objections & Evidentiary Foundations

2021

With amendments through Dec.2020, including FRE 404

Professor John Barkai
William S. Richardson School of Law
University of Hawaii
Honolulu, HI

What's upfront? Traditionally, the first few pages of a book include information about formatting, copyright, dedication, and other such topics before getting to the substance of the text. However, because the unique and most valuable sections in this handbook (objections & foundations) follow the rules section, and because Amazon's "Look inside" feature does not show samples sections of later pages which might make this handbook most attractive to you, I will place some sample pages of the objections and foundations material upfront directly after the content/index pages.

Regarding copyright – there is none. Of course, there is no claim to copyright the Federal Rules of Evidence, a government publication. In addition, I give you permission to freely copy and use other sections of this handbook, including the sections on objections and evidentiary foundations, under a Creative Commons Attribution (CCBY) 4.0 License, which essentially means that you may use, share, or adapt the information in these pages for any purpose, even commercial, if you give "appropriate credit" and indicate changes you made, if any. Please cite the material as: John Barkai, Federal Rules of Evidence Handbook with Common Objections & Evidentiary Foundations (2020). Also, you cannot restrict others from using these materials. However, all cartoons are used in this handbook with permission of the artists, their families, their estates, or the organization that owns their copyrights. You do not have permission to use the cartoons other than those created by John Barkai and / or Mallory Hee (my research assistant who drew some of the cartoons). However, it you are using them for a non-commercial teaching or training purpose, you may be covered by the "fair use" doctrine. Consult a lawyer. You probably know some.

Formatting. There seems to be no standard formatting style for presenting the rules of evidence. This handbook uses formatting intended to make the understanding and application of the rules as clear as possible - but clarity and ease of understanding of the rules of evidence by using the text alone is almost impossible. Font may vary, using larger fonts for rules you are likely to consult more often and smaller fonts for rules less likely to be consulted. Some key words are underlined for emphasis.

Disclaimer: The author and publisher are offering no legal advice. Your trial judge may view the law and foundations differently. The law is whatever the judge in your case says it is. Any errors in this book are mine.

Corrections, omissions, suggestions?
See any or have some? Contact me at barkai@hawaii.edu

Common Citation Forms: Fed. R. Evid. xxx or even FRE xxx.

Federal Rules of Evidence Handbook
with Common Objections & Evidentiary Foundations

ISBN: 9781721104246

INTRODUCTION

This Federal Rules of Evidence Handbook was designed to be brought to court and be at your side in the office.

All FRE books contain the rules of evidence. The **"added value"** in this book is the following useful and entertaining sections:

A) **Making and Responding to Common Objections** (over 15 pages)
- **a discussion of the most common objections**
- **a list of the most common objections**
B) **Evidentiary Foundations and Impeachment** (over 60 pages)
- **more than 25 examples of the most common evidentiary foundations**
- **a brief discussion of differing standards for authenticating digital evidence** (such as email, text messages, social media sites, internet cites)
C) **A humor section with over 20 cartoons and 100 original captions on the topics of trial evidence, negotiations, and ADR.**

The objections and evidentiary foundations sections make this handbook a great resource for clinics, trial practice courses, and mock trial competitors.

The sample foundation and impeachment questions are "bare-bones" foundations which include the minimum questions and answers necessary to get testimony or exhibits admitted into evidence

This handbook does not contain the Advisory Committee Notes to the Federal Rules of Evidence. My evidence students hardly ever consult them, so I doubt you will either. Besides, they are not hard to find on the internet.

Professor John Barkai

Summary of Contents

Appendix

Expanded Table of Contents in the Appendix

Evidentiary Foundations..A-17

Make an Objection in Four Steps
1) Stand up.
2) Say, "Objection ____ " (Fill in the blank with your reason).
3) Identify your specific objection.
   a) At a minimum, say the topic type
      (Hearsay, Relevance, Improper Impeachment, Improper
      Character, Lack of Foundation, Leading Question, etc.)
   b) State the evidence rule number if you know it (404, 608, etc.).
   c) A combination of the above
      ("Objection, Improper Impeachment, R613")
4) Stop talking and listen to the judge.
   Be prepared to state reasons for your objection and to make an
   argument to support your position.

How to Respond to An Objection?
1) Speak to the judge, not the lawyer who objected.
2) Explain to the judge why your evidence should be admissible.
   ("Your Honor, that statement is not hearsay because I am not
   offering it for the truth but rather to show notice.")
3) If you recognize that you did not lay an appropriate foundation
for the evidence explain that you will do that. ("Your Honor, I will
lay the foundation.")
4) If you recognize that the opposing counsel was objecting to the
form of your question, which most often happens on your direct
examination, simply say, "I'll rephrase." Rephrase the question and
move on with your witness examination. Do not get sidetracked by
the opposing counsel who might have objected just to throw you off
track.
5) For any physical piece of evidence, statement, or testimony that
you will be introducing, prepare in advance and have a reason why
you believe that evidence is admissible. Be ready to make that
argument to the judge.
6) If the objection is to relevance, and you think you will be able to
show that it is relevant, say to the judge "I will connect it up in a few
questions Your Honor." Such a statement is equivalent of saying
"trust me." If you do that, you'd better connect it up or the judge
will not trust you in the future.

A List of Common Possible Objections

Ambiguous	Improper opinion
Argumentative	Improper rehabilitation
Asked and answered	Inadmissible opinion
Assumes facts not in evidence	Incompetent witness
Authentication	Incomplete Inflammatory
Badgering	Insufficient foundation
Best evidence	Irrelevant (Relevance)
Beyond the scope	Lack of foundation
Bias	Lack of personal knowledge
Bolstering	Leading question
Calls for a conclusion	Misleading
Calls for speculation	Misquotes a witness or exhibit
Chain of custody	Misquotes evidence
Collateral	Misstates witness
Competence	More prejudicial than probative
Compound question	Motion to strike
Compromise / Settlement offer	Narrative
Confrontation (lack of)	(Question calls for a narrative)
Confusing	Narrative answer
Counsel is testifying	Non-responsive
Cumulative	Nothing pending
Document speaks for itself	Outside the scope of cross
Expert (Improper opinion)	Overly broad or general
Expert (not qualified)	Parole evidence rule
Habit	Personal knowledge
Harassing the witness	Prejudice (unfair)
Hearsay	Privilege communication
Hypothetical question misused	Relevance
Improper character evidence	Speculation/ Opinion/ Lack of
Improper characterization	personal knowledge
Improper impeachment	Unintelligible
	Vague

There are many more possible objections,
limited only by the lawyer's imagination.

Judges and the local legal culture in your jurisdiction may have
other rules or approaches to objections that are not touched on in
this handbook. Ask around and learn about them.

Steps for Introducing Exhibits

Preliminary steps are:
1) Have the exhibit marked for identification
2) Show the proposed exhibit to opposing counsel
3) Ask permission to approach the witness with the proposed exhibit

1. History - How the witness knows the exhibit.

Offer some testimony that the witness <u>knows</u> or is <u>familiar with</u> the evidence – such as a document, physical item, photo, diagram, scene, text message, email - or recalls the statement. Even if the witness has only seen the exhibit once before or has just been to the scene shown in the photograph once before, <u>once is enough</u>.

2. The Litany (a ritualistic repetition of foundational questions)

a) Ask the court clerk to **mark the item** (using numbers or letters). The clerk will decide which system to use. In more serious cases in the jurisdiction's higher courts (typically where jury trials are allowed), exhibits are usually required to be marked at least before trial starts, and often during pretrial conferences.

b) **Show opposing counsel** (this will prevent interruptions) and say, "Let the record reflect that I am showing the defense what has been marked as plaintiff's proposed exhibit number one."

c) Ask the judge for **permission to approach** the witness. "May I approach the witness?"

- Q: "**I show you what has been marked as** Plaintiff's (Prosecution's) (Defense's) proposed exhibit # x (or exhibit #x for identification purposes) **and ask whether you can identify it**" (You expect a "yes" answer here.)

- Q: "**What is it?**" (They describe it in general terms. "It is the contract/photo of the scene/weapon recovered/drugs seized/diagram of the area/etc.")

- Q: "**How do you know that?**" (They answer – "I recognize it. It has my signature on it. / I have been there many times before. / I put my initials on it and the defendant's name/etc.")

3. Show Condition or Comparison or Accuracy

Some comparison must be made between the exhibit in court and when the witness became familiar with the exhibit out-of-court. Of the examples that follow, only one such question is necessary.

- "Is this in the **same** condition as when you... [first saw it...seized it...etc.]?"
- "Is this in the **same or substantially** the same condition.... as when you…"   (for item or document)
- "Is it a **fair and accurate representation** of the ... **as it was that day?**"   (for diagram or pictures)
- "**Has it changed** in any significant way?"
- "**How does it compare** to the item you saw that day?"

4. Move or Offer the Exhibit into Evidence

"Your honor, **I offer the exhibit into evidence**." - or, "I move the exhibit into evidence."

You could instead say, "I offer proposed exhibit # 1 into evidence as exhibit # 1," but why make it so confusing? Just say, "I offer the exhibit into evidence."

The judge <u>might</u> ask the opposing counsel, "Any objections?" but the opponent should object immediately after the proponent offers the exhibit if there is an objection to the admissibility (not the weight). The judge should allow "voir dire" (immediate cross examination limited to the foundation and the admissibility) by the opponent of the exhibit.

Authentication of Text Message – An Example

Text Message

Received by Witness

Do you know Y?

Do you communicate with Y on a regular basis?

In what ways to you communicate with Y?

Did you receive a text message from the Y [recently; on or about _ date, on the topic of …, etc.]?

Would you recognize a printout of the message if you were to see it again?

Let me show you what has been marked as proposed exhibit # 1. Do you recognize it?

What is it? [Ans: A screenshot from my cell phone]

How do you know that this is a message from Y? [It is similar to other messages I have received from Y in that …]

How did it appear when it arrived on your phone? [Showed up under the name and with the picture I had previously assigned to Y]

What other distinctive characteristics did you notice about the message? [provide as many as distinctive characteristics possible]

Is it a fair and accurate representation of the text message you received [recently; on or about _ date, on the topic of visiting your son, etc.]?

Has it been altered in any way?

I would like to enter the proposed exhibit into evidence

From, Humor in Trial Evidence:
Cartoon Caption Contest Winners, by John Barkai (2020)

Artist Misha Richter

"What a coincidence, my lawyer had Barkai for evidence too!"

"You know Larry, I don't think I'd make the best character witness for you."

"My lawyer was wrong! That stuff was admissible the whole time."

P1: "We should hang sometime."
P2: "Yeah. What your cell number?"

"So, it turns out the right to confront witnesses against you doesn't include threatening them with a gun."

"Well if we've learned anything, I guess we shouldn't have updated our escape route on twitter and Facebook."

Artist Joseph Mirachi

"Crawford...Smawford. Let's just admit it!" (confrontation)

"He must be one of Barkai's evidence students."

"Shall we take judicial notice that this lawyer has no idea what he is talking about?" R201

"Thanks to rule 403, we've still got time for a round of golf this afternoon."

"Do you remember how we decided whether the statement was testimonial or not testimonial last time? Was it darts or a coin toss?" (confrontation)

From, Humor in Trial Evidence:
Cartoon Caption Contest Winners, by John Barkai (2020)

Artist Rex May

"So apparently these days the spousal testimonial privilege belongs only to the testifying spouse." R505

"We should have studied more for the evidence exam!"

"I thought grand jury testimony was admissible under a hearsay exception. Crawford changed that?"

"This isn't what I thought the judge meant when she talked about the "chain of custody." R901

"With all those evidence rules, you'd think they'd get us out of here with one of them!"

SAMPLE PAGE FROM DEEPER IN THE HANDBOOK

From, Humor in Trial Evidence:
Cartoon Caption Contest Winners, by John Barkai (2020)

Artist Mallory Hee (my research assistant)

"Can we take judicial notice that the bar results are out, and new lawyers will soon appear before us making bad objections?" R201, R103

"Who are we to judge?"

"They "restyled" the rules of evidence. Don't you think it's time they restyled the robes?"

"Do you remember the difference between adjudicative facts and legislative facts?" R201

J1: "He has a habit of getting on my nerves."
J2: "No, that's just his character." R404, R406

"Psst … I still don't understand hearsay." R801

J1: "He has a habit of getting on my nerves."
J2: "No, that's just his character." R404, R406

The Most Commonly Used
Federal Rules of Evidence Hearsay Sub-Sections

FEDERAL RULES OF EVIDENCE
RULES OF EVIDENCE FOR UNITED STATES COURTS AND MAGISTRATES

ARTICLE I. GENERAL PROVISIONS

Rule 101. Scope; Definitions
(a) Scope. These rules apply to proceedings in United States courts. The specific courts and proceedings to which the rules apply, along with exceptions, are set out in Rule 1101.
(b) Definitions. In these rules
    (1) "civil case" means a civil action or proceeding;
    (2) "criminal case" includes a criminal proceeding;
    (3) "public office" includes a public agency;
    (4) "record" includes a memorandum, report, or data compilation;
    (5) a "rule prescribed by the Supreme Court" means a rule adopted by the Supreme Court under statutory authority; and
    (6) a reference to any kind of written material or any other medium includes electronically stored information.

Rule 102. Purpose
These rules should be construed so as to administer every proceeding fairly, eliminate unjustifiable expense and delay, and promote the development of evidence law, to the end of ascertaining the truth and securing a just determination.

Rule 103. Rulings on Evidence
(a) Preserving a Claim of Error. A party may claim error in a ruling to admit or exclude evidence only if the error affects a substantial right of the party and:
(1) if the ruling admits evidence, a party, on the record:
    (A) timely objects or moves to strike; and
    (B) states the specific ground, unless it was apparent from the context; or
(2) if the ruling excludes evidence, a party informs the court of its substance by an offer of proof, unless the substance was apparent from the context.
(b) Not Needing to Renew an Objection or Offer of Proof. Once the court rules definitively on the record — either before or at trial — a party need not renew an objection or offer of proof to preserve a claim of error for appeal.
(c) Court's Statement About the Ruling; Directing an Offer of Proof. The court may make any statement about the character or form of the evidence, the objection made, and the ruling. The court may direct that an offer of proof be made in question-and-answer form.
(d) Preventing the Jury from Hearing Inadmissible Evidence. To the extent practicable, the court must conduct a jury trial so that inadmissible evidence is not suggested to the jury by any means.
(e) Taking Notice of Plain Error. A court may take notice of a plain error affecting a substantial right, even if the claim of error was not properly preserved.

1

Rule 104. Preliminary Questions

(a) In General. The court must decide any preliminary question about whether a witness is qualified, a privilege exists, or evidence is admissible. In so deciding, the <u>court is not bound by evidence rules, except those on privilege.</u>

(b) Relevance That Depends on a Fact. When the relevance of evidence depends on whether a fact exists, proof must be introduced <u>sufficient to support a finding</u> that the fact does exist. The court may admit the proposed evidence on the condition that the proof be introduced later.

(c) Conducting a Hearing So That the Jury Cannot Hear It. The court must conduct any hearing on a preliminary question so that the jury cannot hear it if:

(1) the hearing involves the admissibility of a confession;

(2) a defendant in a criminal case is a witness and so requests; or

(3) justice so requires.

(d) Cross-Examining a Defendant in a Criminal Case. By testifying on a preliminary question, a defendant in a criminal case does not become subject to cross-examination on other issues in the case.

(e) Evidence Relevant to Weight and Credibility. This rule does not limit a party's right to introduce before the jury evidence that is relevant to the weight or credibility of other evidence.

Rule 105. Limiting Evidence That Is Not Admissible Against Other Parties or for Other Purposes

If the court admits evidence that is admissible against a party or for a purpose — but not against another party or for another purpose — the court, on timely request, must restrict the evidence to its proper scope and instruct the jury accordingly.

Rule 106. Remainder of or Related Writings or Recorded Statements

If a party introduces all or part of a writing or recorded statement, an adverse party may require the introduction, <u>at that time</u>, of any other part — or any other writing or recorded statement — that in fairness ought to be considered at the same time.

ARTICLE II. JUDICIAL NOTICE

Rule 201. Judicial Notice of Adjudicative Facts

(a) Scope. This rule governs judicial notice of an adjudicative fact only, not a legislative fact.

(b) Kinds of Facts That May Be Judicially Noticed. The court may judicially notice a fact that is not subject to reasonable dispute because it:

    (1) is generally known within the trial court's territorial jurisdiction; or

    (2) can be accurately and readily determined from sources whose accuracy cannot reasonably be questioned.

(c) Taking Notice. The court:

    (1) may take judicial notice on its own; or

    (2) must take judicial notice if a party requests it and the court is supplied with the necessary information.

(d) Timing. The court may take judicial notice at any stage of the proceeding.

(e) Opportunity to Be Heard. On timely request, a party is entitled to be heard on the propriety of taking judicial notice and the nature of the fact to be noticed. If the court takes judicial notice before notifying a party, the party, on request, is still entitled to be heard.

(f) Instructing the Jury. In a civil case, the court must instruct the jury to accept the noticed fact as conclusive. In a criminal case, the court must instruct the jury that it may or may not accept the noticed fact as conclusive.

ARTICLE III. PRESUMPTIONS IN CIVIL CASES

Rule 301. Presumptions in Civil Actions Generally

In a civil case, unless a federal statute or these rules provide otherwise, the party against whom a presumption is directed has the burden of producing evidence to rebut the presumption. But this rule does not shift the burden of persuasion, which remains on the party who had it originally.

Rule 302. Applying State Law to Presumptions in Civil Cases

In a civil case, state law governs the effect of a presumption regarding a claim or defense for which state law supplies the rule of decision.

ARTICLE IV. RELEVANCE AND ITS LIMITS

Rule 401. Test for Relevant Evidence
Evidence is relevant if:
(a) it has any tendency to make a fact more or less probable than it would be without the evidence; and
(b) the fact is of consequence in determining the action.

Rule 402. General Admissibility of Relevant Evidence
Relevant evidence is admissible unless any of the following provides otherwise:
- the United States Constitution;
- a federal statute;
- these rules; or
- other rules prescribed by the Supreme Court.

Irrelevant evidence is not admissible.

Rule 403. Excluding Relevant Evidence for Prejudice, Confusion, Waste of Time, or Other Reasons
The court may exclude relevant evidence if its probative value is substantially outweighed by a danger of one or more of the following: unfair prejudice, confusing the issues, misleading the jury, undue delay, wasting time, or needlessly presenting cumulative evidence.

FRE 404 went into effect in Dec. 2020

Rule 404. Character Evidence; <u>Other</u> Crimes, <u>Wrongs</u> or Acts
(a) Character Evidence.
(1) Prohibited Uses. Evidence of a person's character or character trait is not admissible to prove that on a particular occasion the person acted in accordance with the character or trait.
(2) Exceptions for a Defendant or Victim in a Criminal Case. The following exceptions apply in a criminal case:
(A) a defendant may offer evidence of the defendant's pertinent trait, and if the evidence is admitted, the prosecutor may offer evidence to rebut it;
(B) subject to the limitations in Rule 412, a defendant may offer evidence of an alleged victim's pertinent trait, and if the evidence is admitted, the prosecutor may:
    (i) offer evidence to rebut it; and
    (ii) offer evidence of the defendant's same trait; and
(C) in a homicide case, the prosecutor may offer evidence of the alleged victim's trait of peacefulness to rebut evidence that the victim was the first aggressor.
(3) Exceptions for a Witness. Evidence of a witness's character may be admitted under Rules 607, 608, and 609.
(b) Other Crimes, Wrongs, or Acts.
(1) Prohibited Uses. Evidence of any other crime, wrong, or act is not admissible to prove a person's character in order to show that on a particular occasion the person acted in accordance with the character.
(2) Permitted Uses. This evidence may be admissible for another purpose, such as proving motive, opportunity, intent, preparation, plan, knowledge,
identity, absence of mistake, or lack of accident.
(3) Notice in a Criminal Case. In a criminal case, the prosecutor must:
    (A) provide reasonable notice of any such evidence that the prosecutor intends to offer at trial;
    (B) <u>articulate in the notice the non-propensity purpose for which the prosecutor</u>
    <u>intends to offer the evidence and the reasoning that supports the purpose; and</u>
    (C) do so in writing sufficiently ahead of trial to give the defendant a fair opportunity to meet the evidence — or in any form during trial if the court, for
    good cause, excuses lack of pretrial notice.

Rule 405. Methods of Proving Character
(a) By Reputation or Opinion. When evidence of a person's character or character trait is admissible, it may be proved by testimony about the person's <u>reputation</u> or by testimony in the form of an <u>opinion</u>. On cross-examination of the character witness, the court may allow an inquiry into <u>relevant specific instances</u> of the person's conduct.
(b) By Specific Instances of Conduct. When a person's character or character trait is an <u>essential element of a charge, claim, or defense</u>, the character or trait may also be proved by relevant specific instances of the person's conduct.

Rule 406. Habit; Routine Practice
Evidence of a person's habit or an organization's routine practice may be admitted to prove that on a particular occasion the person or organization acted in accordance with the habit or routine practice. The court may admit this evidence regardless of whether it is corroborated or whether there was an eyewitness.

Rule 407. Subsequent Remedial Measures
When measures are taken that would have made an earlier injury or harm less likely to occur, evidence of the subsequent measures is not admissible to prove:
- negligence;
- culpable conduct;
- a defect in a product or its design; or
- a need for a warning or instruction.

But the court may admit this evidence for another purpose, such as <u>impeachment</u> or — if disputed — proving <u>ownership, control, or the feasibility of precautionary measures.</u>

Rule 408. Compromise Offers and Negotiations
(a) Prohibited uses. Evidence of the following is not admissible — on behalf of any party — either to prove or disprove the validity or amount of a disputed claim or to impeach by a prior inconsistent statement or a contradiction:
(1) furnishing, promising, or offering — or accepting, promising to accept, or offering to accept — a valuable consideration in compromising or attempting to compromise the claim; and
(2) conduct or a <u>statement</u> made during compromise negotiations about the claim — except when offered in a criminal case and when the negotiations related to a claim by a public office in the exercise of its regulatory, investigative, or enforcement authority.

(b) Exceptions. The court may admit this evidence for another purpose, such as proving a witness's bias or prejudice, negating a contention of undue delay, or proving an effort to obstruct a criminal investigation or prosecution.

Rule 409. Offers to Pay Medical and Similar Expenses

Evidence of furnishing, promising to pay, or offering to pay medical, hospital, or similar expenses resulting from an injury is not admissible to prove liability for the injury.

Rule 410. Pleas, Plea Discussions, and Related Statements

(a) **Prohibited Uses.** In a civil or criminal case, evidence of the following is not admissible against the defendant who made the plea or participated in the plea discussions:

(1) a guilty plea that was later withdrawn;

(2) a nolo contendere plea;

(3) a statement made during a proceeding on either of those pleas under Federal Rule of Criminal Procedure 11 or a comparable state procedure; or

(4) a statement made during plea discussions with an attorney for the prosecuting authority if the discussions did not result in a guilty plea or they resulted in a later-withdrawn guilty plea.

(b) Exceptions. The court may admit a statement described in Rule 410(a)(3) or (4):

(1) in any proceeding in which another statement made during the same plea or plea discussions has been introduced, if in fairness the statements ought to be considered together; or

(2) in a criminal proceeding for perjury or false statement, if the defendant made the statement under oath, on the record, and with counsel present.

Rule 411. Liability Insurance

Evidence that a person was or was not insured against liability is not admissible to prove whether the person acted negligently or otherwise wrongfully. But the court may admit this evidence for another purpose, such as proving a witness's bias or prejudice or proving agency, ownership, or control.

Rule 412. Sex-Offense Cases: The Victim's Sexual Behavior or Predisposition

(a) Prohibited Uses. The following evidence is not admissible in a civil or criminal proceeding involving alleged sexual misconduct:

(1) evidence offered to prove that a victim engaged in other sexual behavior; or

(2) evidence offered to prove a victim's sexual predisposition.

(b) Exceptions

(1) Criminal Cases. The court may admit the following evidence in a criminal case:

(A) evidence of specific instances of a victim's sexual behavior, if offered to prove that someone other than the defendant was the source of semen, injury, or other physical evidence;

(B) evidence of specific instances of a victim's sexual behavior with respect to the person accused of the sexual misconduct, if offered by the defendant to prove consent or if offered by the prosecutor; and

(C) evidence whose exclusion would violate the defendant's constitutional rights.

(2) Civil Cases. In a civil case, the court may admit evidence offered to prove a victim's sexual behavior or sexual predisposition if its probative value substantially outweighs the danger of harm to any victim and of unfair prejudice to any party. The court may admit evidence of a victim's reputation only if the victim has placed it in controversy.

(c) Procedure to Determine Admissibility

(1) Motion. If a party intends to offer evidence under Rule 412(b), the party must:

(A) file a motion that specifically describes the evidence and states the purpose for which it is to be offered;

(B) do so at least 14 days before trial unless the court, for good cause, sets a different time;

(C) serve the motion on all parties; and

(D) notify the victim or, when appropriate, the victim's guardian or representative.

(2) Hearing. Before admitting evidence under this rule, the court must conduct an in camera hearing and give the victim and parties a right to attend and be heard. Unless the court orders otherwise, the motion, related materials, and the record of the hearing must be and remain sealed.

(d) Definition of "Victim." In this rule, "victim" includes an alleged victim.

Rule 413. Similar Crimes in Sexual-Assault Cases

(a) Permitted Uses. In a criminal case in which a defendant is accused of a sexual assault, the court may admit evidence that the defendant committed any other sexual assault. The evidence may be considered on any matter to which it is relevant.

(b) Disclosure to the Defendant. If the prosecutor intends to offer this evidence, the prosecutor must disclose it to the defendant, including witnesses' statements or a summary of the expected testimony. The prosecutor must do so at least 15 days before trial or at a later time that the court allows for good cause.

(c) Effect on Other Rules. This rule does not limit the admission or consideration of evidence under any other rule.

(d) Definition of "Sexual Assault." In this rule and Rule 415, "sexual assault" means a crime under federal law or under state law (as "state" is defined in 18 U.S.C. § 513) involving:

(1) any conduct prohibited by 18 U.S.C. chapter 109A;

(2) contact, without consent, between any part of the defendant's body — or an object — and another person's genitals or anus;

(3) contact, without consent, between the defendant's genitals or anus and any part of another person's body;

(4) deriving sexual pleasure or gratification from inflicting death, bodily injury, or physical pain on another person; or

(5) an attempt or conspiracy to engage in conduct described in subparagraphs (1)-(4).

Rule 414. Similar Crimes in Child-Molestation Cases

(a) Permitted Uses. In a criminal case in which a defendant is accused of child molestation, the court <u>may admit</u> evidence that the defendant committed any other child molestation. The evidence may be considered on any matter to which it is relevant.

(b) Disclosure to the Defendant. If the prosecutor intends to offer this evidence, the prosecutor must disclose it to the defendant, including witnesses' statements or a summary of the expected testimony. The prosecutor must do so at least 15 days before trial or at a later time that the court allows for good cause.

(c) Effect on Other Rules. This rule does not limit the admission or consideration of evidence under any other rule.

(d) Definition of "Child" and "Child Molestation." In this rule and Rule 415:

(1) "child" means a person below the age of 14; and

(2) "child molestation" means a crime under federal law or under state law (as "state" is defined in 18 U.S.C. § 513) involving:

(A) any conduct prohibited by 18 U.S.C. chapter 109A and committed with a child;

(B) any conduct prohibited by 18 U.S.C. chapter 110;

(C) contact between any part of the defendant's body — or an object — and a child's genitals or anus;

(D) contact between the defendant's genitals or anus and any part of a child's body;

(E) deriving sexual pleasure or gratification from inflicting death, bodily injury, or physical pain on a child; or

(F) an attempt or conspiracy to engage in conduct described in subparagraphs (A)–(E).

Rule 415. Similar Acts in Civil Cases Involving Sexual Assault or Child Molestation

(a) Permitted Uses. (a)In a civil case involving a claim for relief based on a party's alleged sexual assault or child molestation, the court <u>may admit</u> evidence that the party committed any other sexual assault or child molestation. The evidence may be considered as provided in Rules 413 and 414.

(b) Disclosure to the Opponent. If a party intends to offer this evidence, the party must disclose it to the party against whom it will be offered, including witnesses' statements or a summary of the expected testimony. The party must do so at least 15 days before trial or at a later time that the court allows for good cause.

(c) Effect on Other Rules. This rule does not limit the admission or consideration of evidence under any other rule.

ARTICLE V. PRIVILEGES

Rule 501. Privileges in General

The common law — as interpreted by United States courts in the light of reason and experience — governs a claim of privilege unless any of the following provides otherwise:

- the United States Constitution;
- a federal statute; or
- rules prescribed by the Supreme Court.

But in a civil case, state law governs privilege regarding a claim or defense for which state law supplies the rule of decision.

Rule 502. Attorney-Client Privilege and Work Product; Limitations on Waiver

The following provisions apply, in the circumstances set out, to disclosure of a communication or information covered by the attorney-client privilege or work-product protection.

(a) Disclosure Made in a Federal Proceeding or to a Federal Office or Agency; Scope of a Waiver. When the disclosure is made in a federal proceeding or to a federal office or agency and waives the attorney-client privilege or work-product protection, the waiver extends to an undisclosed communication or information in a federal or state proceeding only if:

(1) the waiver is intentional;

(2) the disclosed and undisclosed communications or information concern the same subject matter; and

(3) they ought in fairness to be considered together.

(b) Inadvertent Disclosure. When made in a federal proceeding or to a federal office or agency, the disclosure does not operate as a waiver in a federal or state proceeding if:

(1) the disclosure is inadvertent;

(2) the holder of the privilege or protection took reasonable steps to prevent disclosure; and

(3) the holder promptly took reasonable steps to rectify the error, including (if applicable) following Federal Rule of Civil Procedure 26(b)(5)(B).

(c) Disclosure Made in a State Proceeding. When the disclosure is made in a state proceeding and is not the subject of a state-court order concerning waiver, the disclosure does not operate as a waiver in a federal proceeding if the disclosure

(1) would not be a waiver under this rule if it had been made in a federal proceeding; or

(2) is not a waiver under the law of the State where the disclosure occurred.

(d) Controlling Effect of a Court Order. A federal court may order that the privilege or protection is not waived by disclosure connected with the litigation pending before the court--in which event the disclosure is also not a waiver in any other federal or state proceeding.

(e) Controlling Effect of a Party Agreement. An agreement on the effect of disclosure in a federal proceeding is binding only on the parties to the agreement, unless it is incorporated into a court order.

(f) Controlling Effect of This Rule. Notwithstanding Rules 101 and 1101, this rule applies to state proceedings and to federal court-annexed and federal court-mandated arbitration proceedings, in the circumstances set out in the rule. And notwithstanding Rule 501, this rule applies even if State law provides the rule of decision.

(g) Definitions. In this rule:

(1) "attorney-client privilege" means the protection that applicable law provides for confidential attorney-client communications; and

(2) "work-product protection" means the protection that applicable law provides for tangible material (or its intangible equivalent) prepared in anticipation of litigation or for trial.

ARTICLE VI. WITNESSES

Rule 601. Competency to Testify in General
Every person is competent to be a witness unless these rules provide otherwise. But in a civil case, state law governs the witness's competency regarding a claim or defense for which state law supplies the rule of decision.

Rule 602. Need for Personal Knowledge
A witness may testify to a matter only if evidence is introduced sufficient to support a finding that the witness has personal knowledge of the matter. Evidence to prove personal knowledge may consist of the witness's own testimony. This rule does not apply to a witness's expert testimony under Rule 703.

Rule 603. Oath or Affirmation to Testify Truthfully
Before testifying, a witness must give an oath or affirmation to testify truthfully. It must be in a form designed to impress that duty on the witness's conscience.

Rule 604. Interpreter
An interpreter must be qualified and must give an oath or affirmation to make a true translation.

Rule 605. Judge's Competency as a Witness
The presiding judge may not testify as a witness at the trial. A party need not object to preserve the issue.

Rule 606. Juror's Competency as a Witness
(a) At the Trial. A juror may not testify as a witness before the other jurors at the trial. If a juror is called to testify, the court must give a party an opportunity to object outside the jury's presence.
(b) During an Inquiry into the Validity of a Verdict or Indictment.
    (1) Prohibited Testimony or Other Evidence. During an inquiry into the validity of a verdict or indictment, a juror may not testify about any statement made or incident that occurred during the jury's deliberations; the effect of anything on that juror's or another juror's vote; or any juror's mental processes concerning the verdict or indictment. The court may not receive a juror's affidavit or evidence of a juror's statement on these matters.

(2) Exceptions. A juror may testify about whether:
(A) extraneous prejudicial information was improperly brought to the jury's attention;
(B) an outside influence was improperly brought to bear on any juror; or
(C) a mistake was made in entering the verdict on the verdict form.

Rule 607. Who May Impeach a Witness

Any party, including the party that called the witness, may attack the witness's credibility.

Rule 608. A Witness's Character for Truthfulness or Untruthfulness

(a) Reputation or Opinion Evidence. A witness's credibility may be attacked or supported by testimony about the witness's reputation for having a character for truthfulness or untruthfulness, or by testimony in the form of an opinion about that character. But evidence of truthful character is admissible only after the witness's character for truthfulness has been attacked.

(b) Specific Instances of Conduct.
Except for a criminal conviction under Rule 609, extrinsic evidence is not admissible to prove specific instances of a witness's conduct in order to attack or support the witness's character for truthfulness. But the court may, on cross-examination, allow them to be inquired into if they are probative of the character for truthfulness or untruthfulness of:
(1) the witness; or
(2) another witness whose character the witness being cross-examined has testified about.

By testifying on another matter, a witness does not waive any privilege against self-incrimination for testimony that relates only to the witness's character for truthfulness.

Rule 609. Impeachment by Evidence of a Criminal Conviction

(a) In General. The following rules apply to attacking a witness's character for truthfulness by evidence of a criminal conviction:

(1) for a crime that, in the convicting jurisdiction, was punishable by death or by imprisonment for more than one year, the evidence:

(A) must be admitted, subject to Rule 403 , in a civil case or in a criminal case in which the witness is not a defendant; and

(B) must be admitted in a criminal case in which the witness is a defendant, if the probative value of the evidence outweighs its prejudicial effect to that defendant; and

(2) for any crime regardless of the punishment, the evidence must be admitted if the court can readily determine that establishing the elements of the crime required proving — or the witness's admitting — a dishonest act or false statement.

(b) Limit on Using the Evidence After 10 Years. This subdivision (b) applies if more than 10 years have passed since the witness's conviction or release from confinement for it, whichever is later. Evidence of the conviction is admissible only if:

(1) its probative value, supported by specific facts and circumstances, substantially outweighs its prejudicial effect; and

(2) the proponent gives an adverse party reasonable written notice of the intent to use it so that the party has a fair opportunity to contest its use.

(c) Effect of a Pardon, Annulment, or Certificate of Rehabilitation. Evidence of a conviction is not admissible if:

(1) the conviction has been the subject of a pardon, annulment, certificate of rehabilitation, or other equivalent procedure based on a finding that the person has been rehabilitated, and the person has not been convicted of a later crime punishable by death or by imprisonment for more than one year; or

(2) the conviction has been the subject of a pardon, annulment, or other equivalent procedure based on a finding of innocence.

(d) Juvenile Adjudications. Evidence of a juvenile adjudication is admissible under this rule only if:

(1) it is offered in a criminal case;

(2) the adjudication was of a witness other than the defendant;

(3) an adult's conviction for that offense would be admissible to attack the adult's credibility; and

(4) admitting the evidence is necessary to fairly determine guilt or innocence.

(e) Pendency of an Appeal. A conviction that satisfies this rule is admissible even if an appeal is pending. Evidence of the pendency is also admissible.

Rule 610. Religious Beliefs or Opinions
Evidence of a witness's religious beliefs or opinions is not admissible to attack or support the witness's credibility.

Rule 611. Mode and Order of Examining Witnesses and Presenting Evidence
(a) Control by the Court; Purposes. The court should exercise reasonable control over the mode and order of examining witnesses and presenting evidence so as to:
(1) make those procedures effective for determining the truth;
(2) avoid wasting time; and
(3) protect witnesses from harassment or undue embarrassment.
(b) Scope of Cross-Examination. Cross-examination should not go beyond the subject matter of the direct examination and matters affecting the witness's credibility. The court may allow inquiry into additional matters as if on direct examination.
(c) Leading Questions. Leading questions should not be used on direct examination except as necessary to develop the witness's testimony. Ordinarily, the court should allow leading questions:
(1) on cross-examination; and
(2) when a party calls a hostile witness, an adverse party, or a witness identified with an adverse party.

Rule 612. Writing Used to Refresh a Witness's Memory
(a) Scope. This rule gives an adverse party certain options when a witness uses a writing to refresh memory:
(1) while testifying; or
(2) before testifying, if the court decides that justice requires the party to have those options.
(b) Adverse Party's Options; Deleting Unrelated Matter. Unless 18 U.S.C. § 3500 provides otherwise in a criminal case, an adverse party is entitled to have the writing
produced at the hearing,
to inspect it,
to cross-examine the witness about it, and
to introduce in evidence any portion that relates to the witness's testimony.

[rule continues on next page]

If the producing party claims that the writing includes unrelated matter, the court must examine the writing in camera, delete any unrelated portion, and order that the rest be delivered to the adverse party. Any portion deleted over objection must be preserved for the record.

(c) Failure to Produce or Deliver the Writing. If a writing is not produced or is not delivered as ordered, the court may issue any appropriate order. But if the prosecution does not comply in a criminal case, the court must strike the witness's testimony or — if justice so requires — declare a mistrial.

Rule 613. Witness's Prior Statement

(a) Showing or Disclosing the Statement During Examination. When examining a witness about the witness's prior statement, a party need not show it or disclose its contents to the witness. But the party must, on request, show it or disclose its contents to an adverse party's attorney.

(b) Extrinsic Evidence of a Prior Inconsistent Statement. Extrinsic evidence of a witness's prior inconsistent statement is admissible only if the witness is given an opportunity to explain or deny the statement and an adverse party is given an opportunity to examine the witness about it, or if justice so requires. This subdivision (b) does not apply to an opposing party's statement under Rule 801(d)(2).

Rule 614. Court's Calling or Examining a Witness

(a) Calling. The court may call a witness on its own or at a party's request. Each party is entitled to cross-examine the witness.

(b) Examining. The court may examine a witness regardless of who calls the witness.

(c) Objections. A party may object to the court's calling or examining a witness either at that time or at the next opportunity when the jury is not present.

Rule 615. Excluding Witnesses

At a party's request, the court must order witnesses excluded so that they cannot hear other witnesses' testimony. Or the court may do so on its own. But this rule does not authorize excluding:

(a) a party who is a natural person;

(b) an officer or employee of a party that is not a natural person, after being designated as the party's representative by its attorney;

(c) a person whose presence a party shows to be essential to presenting the party's claim or defense; or

(d) a person authorized by statute to be present.

VII. OPINIONS AND EXPERT TESTIMONY

Rule 701. Opinion Testimony by Lay Witnesses
If a witness is not testifying as an expert, testimony in the form of an opinion is limited to one that is:
(a) rationally based on the witness's perception;
(b) helpful to clearly understanding the witness's testimony or to determining a fact in issue; and
(c) not based on scientific, technical, or other specialized knowledge within the scope of Rule 702.

Rule 702. Testimony by Expert Witnesses
A witness who is qualified as an expert by knowledge, skill, experience, training, or education may testify in the form of an opinion or otherwise if:
(a) the expert's scientific, technical, or other specialized knowledge will help the trier of fact to understand the evidence or to determine a fact in issue;
(b) the testimony is based on sufficient facts or data;
(c) the testimony is the product of reliable principles and methods; and
(d) the expert has reliably applied the principles and methods to the facts of the case.

Rule 703. Bases of an Expert's Opinion Testimony
An expert may base an opinion on facts or data in the case that the expert has been made aware of or personally observed. If experts in the particular field would reasonably rely on those kinds of facts or data in forming an opinion on the subject, they need not be admissible for the opinion to be admitted. But if the facts or data would otherwise be inadmissible, the proponent of the opinion may disclose them to the jury only if their probative value in helping the jury evaluate the opinion substantially outweighs their prejudicial effect.

Rule 704. Opinion on an Ultimate Issue
(a) In General — Not Automatically Objectionable. An opinion is not objectionable just because it embraces an ultimate issue.
(b) Exception. In a criminal case, an expert witness must not state an opinion about whether the defendant did or did not have a mental state or condition that constitutes an element of the crime charged or of a defense. Those matters are for the trier of fact alone.

Rule 705. Disclosing the Facts or Data Underlying an Expert's Opinion

Unless the court orders otherwise, an expert may state an opinion — and give the reasons for it — without first testifying to the underlying facts or data. But the expert may be required to disclose those facts or data on cross-examination.

Rule 706. Court-Appointed Expert Witnesses

(a) Appointment Process. On a party's motion or on its own, the court may order the parties to show cause why expert witnesses should not be appointed and may ask the parties to submit nominations. The court may appoint any expert that the parties agree on and any of its own choosing. But the court may only appoint someone who consents to act.

(b) Expert's Role. The court must inform the expert of the expert's duties. The court may do so in writing and have a copy filed with the clerk or may do so orally at a conference in which the parties have an opportunity to participate. The expert:

(1) must advise the parties of any findings the expert makes;

(2) may be deposed by any party;

(3) may be called to testify by the court or any party; and

(4) may be cross-examined by any party, including the party that called the expert.

(c) Compensation. The expert is entitled to a reasonable compensation, as set by the court. The compensation is payable as follows:

(1) in a criminal case or in a civil case involving just compensation under the Fifth Amendment, from any funds that are provided by law; and

(2) in any other civil case, by the parties in the proportion and at the time that the court direct — and the compensation is then charged like other costs.

(d) Disclosing the Appointment to the Jury. The court may authorize disclosure to the jury that the court appointed the expert.

(e) Parties' Choice of Their Own Experts. This rule does not limit a party in calling its own experts

ARTICLE VIII. HEARSAY

Rule 801. Definitions That Apply to This Article; Exclusions from Hearsay

(a) Statement. "Statement" means a person's oral assertion, written assertion, or <u>nonverbal conduct, if the person intended it as an assertion.</u>

(b) Declarant. "Declarant" means the person who made the statement.

(c) Hearsay. "Hearsay" means a statement that:

(1) the declarant does not make while testifying at the current trial or hearing; and

(2) a party offers in evidence to prove the truth of the matter asserted in the statement.

(d) Statements That Are Not Hearsay. A statement that meets the following conditions is <u>not hearsay</u>:

(1) *A* Declarant-Witness's Prior Statement. The declarant <u>testifies</u> and <u>is subject to cross</u>-examination about a prior statement, and the statement:

(A) is <u>inconsistent</u> with the declarant's testimony and was given <u>under penalty of perjury</u> at a trial, hearing, or other proceeding or in a deposition;

(B) is <u>consistent</u> with the declarant's testimony and is offered:

(i) to rebut an express or implied charge that the declarant recently fabricated it or acted from a recent improper influence or motive in so testifying; <u>or</u>

(ii) to rehabilitate the declarant's credibility as a witness when attacked on another ground; or

(C) <u>identifies</u> a person as someone the declarant perceived earlier.

(2) An Opposing Party's Statement. The statement is offered against an opposing party and:

(A) was made by the party in <u>an individual or representative</u> capacity;

(B) is one the party manifested that it <u>adopted or believed</u> to be true;

(C) was made by a person whom the party <u>authorized</u> to make a statement on the subject;

(D) was made by the party's <u>agent</u> or employee on a matter <u>within the scope</u> of that relationship and <u>while it existed</u>; or

(E) was made by the party's <u>coconspirator during and in furtherance</u> of the conspiracy.

The statement must be considered but does not by itself establish the declarant's authority under (C); the existence or scope of the relationship under (D); or the existence of the conspiracy or participation in it under (E).

Rule 802. The Rule Against Hearsay

Hearsay is not admissible unless any of the following provides otherwise:
- a federal statute;
- these rules; or
- other rules prescribed by the Supreme Court.

Rule 803. Exceptions to the Rule Against Hearsay — Regardless of Whether the Declarant Is Available as a Witness

The following are not excluded by the rule against hearsay, regardless of whether the declarant is available as a witness:

(1) Present Sense Impression. A statement describing or explaining an event or condition, made while or immediately after the declarant perceived it.

(2) Excited Utterance. A statement relating to a startling event or condition, made while the declarant was under the stress of excitement that it caused.

(3) Then-Existing Mental, Emotional, or Physical Condition. A statement of the declarant's then-existing state of mind (such as motive, intent, or plan) or emotional, sensory, or physical condition (such as mental feeling, pain, or bodily health), but not including a statement of memory or belief to prove the fact remembered or believed unless it relates to the validity or terms of the declarant's will.

(4) Statement Made for Medical Diagnosis or Treatment. A statement that:

(A) is made for — and is reasonably pertinent to — medical diagnosis or treatment; and

(B) describes medical history; past or present symptoms or sensations; their inception; or their general cause.

(5) Recorded Recollection. A record that:

    (A) is on a matter the witness <u>once knew</u> about but <u>now cannot recall</u> well enough to testify fully and accurately;

    (B) was <u>made or adopted</u> by the witness when the matter was <u>fresh</u> in the witness's memory; and

    (C) <u>accurately reflects</u> the witness's knowledge.

    If admitted, the record may be <u>read</u> into evidence but may be received as an exhibit only if offered by an adverse party.

(6) Records of a Regularly Conducted Activity. A record of an act, event, condition, opinion, or diagnosis if:

    (A) the record was made <u>at or near</u> the time by — or from information transmitted by — <u>someone with knowledge</u>;

    (B) the record was <u>kept</u> in the <u>course of</u> a regularly conducted activity of a business, organization, occupation, or calling, whether or not for profit;

    (C) making the record was a <u>regular practice</u> of that activity;

    (D) all these conditions are shown by the testimony of the custodian or another qualified witness, or by a certification that complies with Rule 902(11) or (12) or with a statute permitting certification; and

    (E) the <u>opponent does not show</u> that the source of information or the method or circumstances of preparation indicate a lack of trustworthiness.

(7) Absence of a Record of a Regularly Conducted Activity. Evidence that a matter is not included in a record described in paragraph (6) if:

    (A) the evidence is admitted to prove that the matter did not occur or exist;

    (B) a record was regularly kept for a matter of that kind; and

    (C) the <u>opponent does not show</u> that the possible source of information <u>or</u> other indicate a lack of trustworthiness.

(8) Public Records. A record or statement of a public office if:
   (A) it sets out:
      (i) the office's <u>activities</u>;
      (ii) a <u>matter observed </u>while under a legal duty to report, but <u>not</u> including, in a <u>criminal</u> case, a matter observed by law-enforcement personnel; or
      (iii) in a <u>civil</u> case or against the government in a criminal case, <u>factual findings</u> from a legally authorized investigation; and
   (B) the <u>opponent does not show</u> that the source of information <u>or</u> other circumstances of preparation indicate a lack of trustworthiness.

(9) Public Records of Vital Statistics. A record of a birth, death, or marriage, if reported to a public office in accordance with a legal duty.

(10) Absence of a Public Record. Testimony — or a certification under Rule 902 [15] — that a diligent search failed to disclose a public record or statement if
   (A) the testimony or certification is admitted to prove that
      (i) the record or statement does not exist;
      or
      (ii) a matter did not occur or exist, if a public office regularly kept a record or statement for a matter of that kind; and
   (B) in a criminal case, a prosecutor who intends to offer a certification provides written notice of that intent at least 14 days before trial, and the defendant does not object in writing within 7 days of receiving the notice — unless the court sets a different time for the notice or the objection.

(11) Records of Religious Organizations Concerning Personal or Family History. A statement of birth, legitimacy, ancestry, marriage, divorce, death, relationship by blood or marriage, or similar facts of personal or family history, contained in a regularly kept record of a religious organization.

(12) Certificates of Marriage, Baptism, and Similar Ceremonies. A statement of fact contained in a certificate:

   (A) made by a person who is authorized by a religious organization or by law to perform the act certified;

   (B) attesting that the person performed a marriage or similar ceremony or administered a sacrament; and

   (C) purporting to have been issued at the time of the act or within a reasonable time after it.

(13) Family Records. A statement of fact about personal or family history contained in a family record, such as a Bible, genealogy, chart, engraving on a ring, inscription on a portrait, or engraving on an urn or burial marker.

(14) Records of Documents That Affect an Interest in Property. The record of a document that purports to establish or affect an interest in property if:

   (A) the record is admitted to prove the content of the original recorded document, along with its signing and its delivery by each person who purports to have signed it;

   (B) the record is kept in a public office; and

   (C) a statute authorizes recording documents of that kind in that office.

(15) Statements in Documents That Affect an Interest in Property. A statement contained in a document that purports to establish or affect an interest in property if the matter stated was relevant to the document's purpose — unless later dealings with the property are inconsistent with the truth of the statement or the purport of the document.

(16) Statements in Ancient Documents. A statement in a document that was prepared before January 1, 1998 and whose authenticity is established.

(17) Market Reports and Similar Commercial Publications. Market quotations, lists, directories, or other compilations that are generally relied on by the public or by persons in particular occupations.

(18) Statements in Learned Treatises, Periodicals, or Pamphlets. A statement contained in a treatise, periodical, or pamphlet if:

(A) the statement is <u>called to the attention</u> of an expert witness on cross-examination <u>or relied on</u> by the expert on direct examination; and

(B) the publication is <u>established as a reliable authority</u> by the expert's admission or testimony, by another expert's testimony, or by judicial notice.

If admitted, the statement may be <u>read</u> into evidence but <u>not received</u> as an exhibit.

(19) Reputation Concerning Personal or Family History. A reputation among a person's family by blood, adoption, or marriage — or among a person's associates or in the community — concerning the person's birth, adoption, legitimacy, ancestry, marriage, divorce, death, relationship by blood, adoption, or marriage, or similar facts of personal or family history.

(20) Reputation Concerning Boundaries or General History. A reputation in a community — arising before the controversy — concerning boundaries of land in the community or customs that affect the land, or concerning general historical events important to that community, state, or nation.

(21) Reputation Concerning Character. A reputation among a person's associates or in the community concerning the person's character.

(22) Judgment of a Previous Conviction. Evidence of a final judgment of conviction if:

> **(A)** the judgment was entered after a trial or guilty plea, but not a nolo contendere plea;
>
> **(B)** the conviction was for a crime punishable by death or by imprisonment for more than a year;
>
> **(C)** the evidence is admitted to prove any fact essential to the judgment; and
>
> **(D)** when offered by the prosecutor in a criminal case for a purpose other than impeachment, the judgment was against the defendant.

The pendency of an appeal may be shown but does not affect admissibility.

(23) Judgments Involving Personal, Family, or General History, or a Boundary. A judgment that is admitted to prove a matter of personal, family, or general history, or boundaries, if the matter:

> **(A)** was essential to the judgment; and
>
> **(B)** could be proved by evidence of reputation.

(24) [Other Exceptions.] [Transferred to Rule 807.]

Rule 804. Exceptions to the Rule Against Hearsay — When the Declarant Is Unavailable as a Witness

(a) Criteria for Being Unavailable. A declarant is considered to be unavailable as a witness if the declarant:

(1) is exempted from testifying about the subject matter of the declarant's statement because the court rules that a privilege applies;

(2) refuses to testify about the subject matter despite a court order to do so;

(3) testifies to not remembering the subject matter;

(4) cannot be present or testify at the trial or hearing because of death or a then-existing infirmity, physical illness, or mental illness; or

(5) is absent from the trial or hearing and the statement's proponent has not been able, by process or other reasonable means, to procure:

(A) the declarant's attendance, in the case of a hearsay exception under Rule 804(b)(1) or (6); or

(B) the declarant's attendance or testimony, in the case of a hearsay exception under Rule 804(b)(2), (3), or (4).

But this subdivision (a) does not apply if the statement's proponent procured or wrongfully caused the declarant's unavailability as a witness in order to prevent the declarant from attending or testifying.

(b) The Exceptions. The following are not excluded by the rule against hearsay if the declarant is unavailable as a witness:

(1) Former Testimony. Testimony that:

(A) was given as a witness at a trial, hearing, or lawful deposition, whether given during the current proceeding or a different one; and

(B) is now offered against a party who had — or, in a civil case, whose predecessor in interest had — an opportunity and similar motive to develop it by direct, cross-, or redirect examination.

(2) Statement Under the Belief of Imminent Death. In a prosecution for homicide or in a civil case, a statement that the declarant, while believing the declarant's death to be imminent, made about its cause or circumstances.

(3) Statement Against Interest. A statement that:

   (A) a reasonable person in the declarant's position would have made only if the person believed it to be true because, when made, it was so contrary to the declarant's proprietary or pecuniary interest or had so great a tendency to invalidate the declarant's claim against someone else or to expose the declarant to civil or criminal liability; and

   (B) is supported by corroborating circumstances that clearly indicate its trustworthiness, if it is offered in a criminal case as one that tends to expose the declarant to criminal liability.

(4) Statement of Personal or Family History. A statement about:

   (A) the declarant's own birth, adoption, legitimacy, ancestry, marriage, divorce, relationship by blood, adoption, or marriage, or similar facts of personal or family history, even though the declarant had no way of acquiring personal knowledge about that fact; or

   (B) another person concerning any of these facts, as well as death, if the declarant was related to the person by blood, adoption, or marriage or was so intimately associated with the person's family that the declarant's information is likely to be accurate.

(5) [Other Exceptions.] [Transferred to Rule 807.]

(6) Statement Offered Against a Party That Wrongfully Caused the Declarant's Unavailability. A statement offered against a party that wrongfully caused — or acquiesced in wrongfully causing — the declarant's unavailability as a witness, and did so intending that result.

Rule 805. Hearsay Within Hearsay

Hearsay within hearsay is not excluded by the rule against hearsay if each part of the combined statements conforms with an exception to the rule.

Rule 806. Attacking and Supporting the Declarant's Credibility

When a hearsay statement — or a statement described in Rule 801(d)(2)(C), (D), or (E) [13] — has been admitted in evidence, the declarant's credibility may be attacked, and then supported, by any evidence that would be admissible for those purposes if the declarant had testified as a witness. The court may admit evidence of the declarant's inconsistent statement or conduct, regardless of when it occurred or whether the declarant had an opportunity to explain or deny it. If the party against whom the statement was admitted calls the declarant as a witness, the party may examine the declarant on the statement as if on cross-examination.

Rule 807. Residual Exception

(a) In General. Under the following conditions, a hearsay statement is not excluded by the rule against hearsay even if the statement is not admissible under a hearsay exception in Rule 803 or 804:

(1) the statement is supported by sufficient guarantees of trustworthiness—after considering the totality of circumstances under which it was made and evidence, if any, corroborating the statement; and

(2) it is more probative on the point for which it is offered than any other evidence that the proponent can obtain through reasonable efforts.

(b) Notice. The statement is admissible only if the proponent gives an adverse party reasonable notice of the intent to offer the statement—including its substance and the declarant's name— so that the party has a fair opportunity to meet it. The notice must be provided in writing before the trial or hearing—or in any form during the trial or hearing of the court, for good cause, excuses a lack of earlier notice.

[Amended in 2019]

ARTICLE IX. AUTHENTICATION AND IDENTIFICATION

Rule 901. Authenticating or Identifying Evidence

(a) In General. To satisfy the requirement of authenticating or identifying an item of evidence, the proponent must produce evidence <u>sufficient to support a finding</u> that the item is what the proponent claims it is.

(b) Examples. The following are examples only — not a complete list — of evidence that satisfies the requirement:

    (1) Testimony of a Witness with Knowledge. Testimony that an item is what it is claimed to be.

    (2) Nonexpert Opinion About Handwriting. A nonexpert's opinion that handwriting is genuine, based on a familiarity with it that was not acquired for the current litigation.

    (3) Comparison by an Expert Witness or the Trier of Fact. A comparison with an authenticated specimen by an expert witness or the trier of fact.

    (4) Distinctive Characteristics and the Like. The appearance, contents, substance, internal patterns, or other distinctive characteristics of the item, taken together with all the circumstances.

    (5) Opinion About a Voice. An opinion identifying a person's voice — whether heard firsthand or through mechanical or electronic transmission or recording — based on hearing the voice at any time under circumstances that connect it with the alleged speaker.

    (6) Evidence About a Telephone Conversation. For a telephone conversation, evidence that a call was made to the number assigned at the time to: **(A)** a particular person, if circumstances, including self-identification, show that the person answering was the one called; or

    (B) a particular business, if the call was made to a business and the call related to business reasonably transacted over the telephone.

    (7) Evidence About Public Records. Evidence that:

      (A) a document was recorded or filed in a public office as authorized by law; or

      (B) a purported public record or statement is from the office where items of this kind are kept.

    (8) Evidence About Ancient Documents or Data Compilations. For a document or data compilation, evidence that it:

      (A) is in a condition that creates no suspicion about its authenticity;

      (B) was in a place where, if authentic, it would likely be; and

      (C) is at least 20 years old when offered.

    (9) Evidence About a Process or System. Evidence describing a process or system and showing that it produces an accurate result.

    (10) Methods Provided by a Statute or Rule. Any method of authentication or identification allowed by a federal statute or a rule prescribed by the Supreme Court.

Rule 902. Evidence That Is Self-Authenticating

The following items of evidence are self-authenticating; they require no extrinsic evidence of authenticity in order to be admitted:

(1) Domestic Public Documents That Are Sealed and Signed. A document that bears:

    (A) a seal purporting to be that of the United States; any state, district, commonwealth, territory, or insular possession of the United States; the former Panama Canal Zone; the Trust Territory of the Pacific Islands; a political subdivision of any of these entities; or a department, agency, or officer of any entity named above; and

    (B) a signature purporting to be an execution or attestation.

(2) Domestic Public Documents That Are Not Sealed but Are Signed and Certified. A document that bears no seal if:

    (A) it bears the signature of an officer or employee of an entity named in Rule 902(1)(A); and

    (B) another public officer who has a seal and official duties within that same entity certifies under seal — or its equivalent — that the signer has the official capacity and that the signature is genuine.

(3) Foreign Public Documents. A document that purports to be signed or attested by a person who is authorized by a foreign country's law to do so. The document must be accompanied by a final certification that certifies the genuineness of the signature and official position of the signer or attester — or of any foreign official whose certificate of genuineness relates to the signature or attestation or is in a chain of certificates of genuineness relating to the signature or attestation. The certification may be made by a secretary of a United States embassy or legation; by a consul general, vice consul, or consular agent of the United States; or by a diplomatic or consular official of the foreign country assigned or accredited to the United States. If all parties have been given a reasonable opportunity to investigate the document's authenticity and accuracy, the court may, for good cause, either:

    (A) order that it be treated as presumptively authentic without final certification; or

    (B) allow it to be evidenced by an attested summary with or without final certification.

(4) Certified Copies of Public Records. A copy of an official record — or a copy of a document that was recorded or filed in a public office as authorized by law — if the copy is certified as correct by:

    (A) the custodian or another person authorized to make the certification; or

    (B) a certificate that complies with Rule 902(1), (2), or (3) , a federal statute, or a rule prescribed by the Supreme Court.

(5) Official Publications. A book, pamphlet, or other publication purporting to be issued by a public authority.

(6) Newspapers and Periodicals. Printed material purporting to be a newspaper or periodical.

(7) Trade Inscriptions and the Like. An inscription, sign, tag, or label purporting to have been affixed in the course of business and indicating origin, ownership, or control.

(8) Acknowledged Documents. A document accompanied by a certificate of acknowledgment that is lawfully executed by a notary public or another officer who is authorized to take acknowledgments.

(9) Commercial Paper and Related Documents. Commercial paper, a signature on it, and related documents, to the extent allowed by general commercial law.

(10) Presumptions Under a Federal Statute. A signature, document, or anything else that a federal statute declares to be presumptively or prima facie genuine or authentic.

(11) Certified Domestic Records of a Regularly Conducted Activity. The original or a copy of a domestic record that meets the requirements of Rule 803(6)(A)-(C), as shown by a certification of the custodian or another qualified person that complies with a federal statute or a rule prescribed by the Supreme Court. Before the trial or hearing, the proponent must give an adverse party reasonable written notice of the intent to offer the record — and must make the record and certification available for inspection — so that the party has a fair opportunity to challenge them.

(12) Certified Foreign Records of a Regularly Conducted Activity. In a civil case, the original or a copy of a foreign record that meets the requirements of Rule 902(11), modified as follows: the certification, rather than complying with a federal statute or Supreme Court rule, must be signed in a manner that, if falsely made, would subject the maker to a criminal penalty in the country where the certification is signed. The proponent must also meet the notice requirements of Rule 902(11).

(13) Certified Records Generated by an Electronic Process or System. A record generated by an electronic process or system that produces an accurate result, as shown by a certification of a qualified person that complies with the certification requirements of Rule 902(11) or (12). The proponent must also meet the notice requirements of Rule 902(11).

(14) Certified Data Copied from an Electronic Device, Storage Medium, or File. Data copied from an electronic device, storage medium, or file, if authenticated by a process of digital identification, as shown by a certification of a qualified person that complies with the certification requirements of Rule 902(11) or (12). The proponent also must meet the notice requirements of Rule 902(11).

Rule 903. Subscribing Witness's Testimony
A subscribing witness's testimony is necessary to authenticate a writing only if required by the law of the jurisdiction that governs its validity.

ARTICLE X. CONTENTS OF WRITINGS, RECORDINGS, AND PHOTOGRAPHS

Rule 1001. Definitions That Apply to This Article

In this article:

(a) A "writing" consists of letters, words, numbers, or their equivalent set down in any form.

(b) A "recording" consists of letters, words, numbers, or their equivalent recorded in any manner.

(c) A "photograph" means a photographic image or its equivalent stored in any form.

(d) An "original" of a writing or recording means the writing or recording itself or any counterpart <u>intended to have</u> the same effect by the person who executed or issued it. For electronically stored information, "original" means <u>any printout</u> — or other output readable by sight — if it accurately reflects the information. An "original" of a photograph includes the negative or a <u>print</u> from it.

(e) A "duplicate" means a counterpart produced by a mechanical, photographic, chemical, electronic, or other equivalent process or technique that accurately reproduces the original.

Rule 1002. Requirement of the Original

An <u>original</u> writing, recording, or photograph <u>is required in order to prove its content</u> unless these rules or a federal statute provides otherwise.

Rule 1003. Admissibility of Duplicates

A <u>duplicate</u> is admissible to the <u>same</u> extent as the <u>original</u> unless a genuine question is raised about the original's authenticity or the circumstances make it unfair to admit the duplicate.

Rule 1004. Admissibility of Other Evidence of Content

An original is not required and other evidence of the content of a writing, recording, or photograph is admissible if:

(a) all the originals are <u>lost or destroyed</u>, and not by the proponent acting in bad faith;

(b) an original <u>cannot be obtained</u> by any available judicial process;

(c) the party against whom the original would be offered had control of the original; was at that time put on notice, by pleadings or otherwise, that the original would be a subject of proof at the trial or hearing; and <u>fails to produce</u> it at the trial or hearing; or

(d) the writing, recording, or photograph is <u>not</u> closely related to a <u>controlling issue</u>.

Rule 1005. Copies of Public Records to Prove Content

The proponent may use a copy to prove the content of an official record — or of a document that was recorded or filed in a public office as authorized by law — if these conditions are met: the record or document is otherwise admissible; and the copy is certified as correct in accordance with Rule 902(4) or is testified to be correct by a witness who has compared it with the original. If no such copy can be obtained by reasonable diligence, then the proponent may use other evidence to prove the content.

Rule 1006. Summaries to Prove Content

The proponent may use a summary, chart, or calculation to prove the content of voluminous writings, recordings, or photographs that cannot be conveniently examined in court. The proponent must make the originals or duplicates available for examination or copying, or both, by other parties at a reasonable time and place. And the court may order the proponent to produce them in court.

Rule 1007. Testimony or Statement of a Party to Prove Content

The proponent may prove the content of a writing, recording, or photograph by the testimony, deposition, or written statement of the party against whom the evidence is offered. The proponent need not account for the original.

Rule 1008. Functions of the Court and Jury

Ordinarily, the court determines whether the proponent has fulfilled the factual conditions for admitting other evidence of the content of a writing, recording, or photograph under Rule 1004 or 1005 . But in a jury trial, the jury determines — in accordance with Rule 104(b) — any issue about whether:

(a) an asserted writing, recording, or photograph ever existed

(b) another one produced at the trial or hearing is the original; or

(c) other evidence of content accurately reflects the content.

ARTICLE XI. MISCELLANEOUS RULES

Rule 1101. Applicability of the Rules
(a) To Courts and Judges. These rules apply to proceedings before:
- United States district courts;
- United States bankruptcy and magistrate judges;
- United States courts of appeals;
- the United States Court of Federal Claims; and
- the district courts of Guam, the Virgin Islands, and the Northern Mariana Islands.

(b) To Cases and Proceedings. These rules apply in:
- civil cases and proceedings, including bankruptcy, admiralty, and maritime cases;
- criminal cases and proceedings; and
- contempt proceedings, except those in which the court may act summarily.

(c) Rules on Privilege. The rules on privilege apply to all stages of a case or proceeding.

(d) Exceptions. These rules — except for those on privilege — do not apply to the following:

(1) the court's determination, under Rule 104(a), on a preliminary question of fact governing admissibility;

(2) grand-jury proceedings; and

(3) miscellaneous proceedings such as:
- extradition or rendition;
- issuing an arrest warrant, criminal summons, or search warrant;
- a preliminary examination in a criminal case;
- sentencing;
- granting or revoking probation or supervised release; and
- considering whether to release on bail or otherwise.

(e) Other Statutes and Rules. A federal statute or a rule prescribed by the Supreme Court may provide for admitting or excluding evidence independently from these rules.

Rule 1102. Amendments
These rules may be amended as provided in 28 U.S.C. § 2072.

Rule 1103. Title
These rules may be cited as the Federal Rules of Evidence.

Making and Responding to Common Objections

Professor John Barkai

> This section of the handbook provides ideas about making and responding to common objections, and it also includes a list of common objections.

There is almost an endless number of objections that could be made at a trial. There are many lists or "cheat sheets" of objections that can be found on the Internet and many articles about objections. This section of the handbook will discuss the basics about objections and provide a list of the more common objections.

Why Do Lawyers Object?

Lawyers object during trial to:

1) control the information that the fact finder can consider
   (to exclude testimony or exhibits offered by the opposing party),

2) control the opposing lawyer's conduct
   (to prevent certain questions or answers, prevent the calling of certain witnesses, prevent certain statements from being made during opening statements or closing arguments),

3) preserve errors for appeal,

4) disrupt opponent's counsel's momentum,

5) send a signal to a witness,

6) communicate with the fact finder, and

7) give the witness a break and time to think.

Lawyers frequently object to the form of question (Argumentative, Ambiguous, Vague, Asked and Answered, etc.) to prevent the judge or jury from hearing inadmissible evidence. Often, however, such objections are made simply to harass, annoy, upset, or distract opposing counsel. The less experience the lawyer doing trials has, the more such objections are likely to distract them. Some people consider objections made for such purposes to be "unethical;" other people consider such objections part of the competition in the adversary system. Whatever your view, be ready for such objections.

Make an Objection in Four Steps

1) Stand up.
2) Say, "Objection ____ " (Fill in the blank with your reason).
3) Identify your specific objection.
    a) At a minimum, say the topic type
        (Hearsay, Relevance, Improper Impeachment, Improper
        Character, Lack of Foundation, Leading Question, etc.)
    b) State the evidence rule number if you know it (404, 608, etc.).
    c) A combination of the above
        ("Objection, Improper Impeachment, R613")
4) Stop talking and listen to the judge.
    Be prepared to state reasons for your objection and to make an
    argument to support your position.

How to Respond to an Objection

1) Speak to the judge, not the lawyer who objected.
2) Explain to the judge why your evidence should be admissible.
    ("Your Honor, that statement is not hearsay because I am not
    offering it for the truth, but rather to show notice.")
3) If you recognize that you did not lay an appropriate foundation
    for the evidence, explain that you will do that. ("Your Honor, I
    will lay the foundation.")
4) If you recognize that the opposing counsel was objecting to the
    form of your question, which most often happens on your direct
    examination, simply say, "I'll rephrase." Rephrase the question
    and move on with your witness examination. Do not get
    sidetracked by the opposing counsel who might have objected
    just to throw you off track.
5) For any physical piece of evidence, statement, or testimony that
    you will be introducing, prepare in advance and have a reason
    why you believe that evidence is admissible. Be ready to make
    that argument to the judge.
6) If the objection is to relevance, and you think you will be able to
    show that it is relevant after additional testimony, say to the
    judge, "I will connect it up in a few questions Your Honor."
    Such a statement is equivalent of saying "trust me." If you do
    say that, you had better connect it up later or the judge will not
    trust you in the future.

If You are a Judge Who Has to Rule on the Objection
1) If the specific objection was not identified, turn to the lawyer who made the objection and say, "Basis?" - Meaning, "What is the legal basis for your objection?"
2) After the lawyer has put their specific objection on the record, turn to the proponent (the lawyer who is attempting to introduce the evidence), and say, "What is your response?"
3) Allow more argument if necessary. "Counsel, how do you respond to that argument?"
4) After the arguments are completed, make your ruling.
   A) "Sustained" - meaning you agree with the objection, and you will exclude the evidence.
   B) "Overruled" - meaning you agree with the proponent of the evidence, and the evidence will be admissible.
   C) Reserve your ruling until the end of the trial. ("I will reserve my decision on this issue until the close of the testimony.")
   D) Ask lawyers to submit a written memorandum on the issue when the trial ends so you have a better understanding of the issue.

Multiple Lawyers and Multiple Clients
If two or more lawyers represent one client, only one of the lawyers can object to each of the witnesses. Only one lawyer can make objections for each witness, e.g. if you do the direct, you are the only one who can object on cross. They cannot "tag team" and both object or respond to objections for single witness. If there are multiple parties who each have their own lawyer, each lawyer must make their own objection to have the objections preserved for appeal.

Judges Apply the Rules of Evidence More Loosely in Nonjury Trials. Many jurisdictions apply a presumption that a trial judge will ignore inadmissible evidence. I doubt that is true. What is to the questionable evidence is very seldom basis for reversing a verdict in a nonjury trial.

The Key to Objection is Rule 103 There is a rhyme to this phrase. "Key" rhymes with "103." Rule 103 holds the key to understanding the process of objections. Read that rule very carefully. The full rule follows.

Important Points about Rule 103 include:

1) The objection must be timely and state the specific ground for the objection, unless it is apparent from the context.

2) If the evidence was admitted, appellate courts do not have to consider the issue unless a specific ground for the objection was timely stated.

3) If the evidence was excluded, the appellate court needs information about what the excluded evidence was going to be. That information must be provided by an "offer of proof" unless the information was apparent from the context.

4) The judge can make statements for the record about the objection, the evidence, the form of the evidence, the ruling, and can require an offer of proof in question and answer form.

5) An error is not sufficient to reverse the trial unless a "substantial right" of a party is affected.

6) Even if there was no objection at trial, "plain errors" affecting "substantial rights" can result in a reversal on appeal.

RULE 103. Rulings on Evidence

(a) Preserving a Claim of Error. A party may claim error in a ruling to admit or exclude evidence only if the error affects a substantial right of the party and:

    (1) if the ruling admits evidence, a party, on the record:

        (A) timely objects or moves to strike; and

        (B) states the specific ground, unless it was apparent from the context; or

    (2) if the ruling excludes evidence, a party informs the court of its substance by an offer of proof, unless the substance was apparent from the context.

(b) Not Needing to Renew an Objection or Offer of Proof. Once the court rules definitively on the record — either before or at trial — a party need not renew an objection or offer of proof to preserve a claim of error for appeal.

(c) Court's Statement About the Ruling; Directing an Offer of Proof. The court may make any statement about the character or form of the evidence, the objection made, and the ruling. The court may direct that an offer of proof be made in question-and-answer form.

(d) Preventing the Jury from Hearing Inadmissible Evidence. To the extent practicable, the court must conduct a jury trial so that inadmissible evidence is not suggested to the jury by any means.

(e) Taking Notice of Plain Error. A court may take notice of a plain error affecting a substantial right, even if the claim of error was not properly preserved.

The Most Common Substantive Objections Are Based on The Rules of Evidence and Constitutional Issues. Each article within the evidence code has one or more common types of objections, such as:

General provisions	100s
Objections	
Preliminary questions	
Limited admissibility	
Remainder of or related writings	
Judicial notice	200s
Presumptions	300s
Relevance	400s
Privileges	500s
Witnesses	600s
Competence	
Impeachment	
Opinions and expert testimony	700s
Hearsay	800s
Authentication	900s
Best evidence (original writings)	1000s

Motions in Limine

In a jury trial, lawyers often make a pretrial motion in limine, which is a motion to exclude or admit certain evidence. In jury trials, the motion is made outside the presence of the jury. The judge's ruling on the motion in limine can 1) prevent inadmissible evidence from being heard by a jury, or 2) allow lawyers to know that they can go forward and attempt to introduce certain evidence without risking a mistrial. Motions in limine are probably not necessary in a nonjury trial because the judge will have to hear the potentially inadmissible evidence before ruling on the motion. Therefore, even if the evidence would be ruled inadmissible, the trial judge who will be the trier of fact will have already heard the inadmissible evidence. Judges in nonjury trials are presumed to ignore inadmissible evidence.

Phrases and Questions that Suggest Inadmissible or Objectionable Information is Coming.

Lawyer: "In summary, witness you've testified that…"
Likely objection: Asked and answered

Lawyer: "Witness, what if I told you that another witness testified that…"
Likely objection: Calls for speculation, argumentative, etc.

Inadequate Objections – Not Specific Enough
"I object."
"Objection to the form of the question."
"Insufficient foundation."
"Inadmissible."
"Incompetent, irrelevant, and immaterial."

Offers of Proof are:
1) sometimes just summary statements by a lawyer of what the evidence would be if the lawyer were given an opportunity to call the witness or introduce the exhibit. ("Your Honor, if the witness would be allowed to testify, she would say that ……"), and,
2) sometimes offers of proof are questions of the lawyer and answers of the witness given in question and answer form outside the presence of the jury. (Q1 A1; Q2 A2; Q3 A3)

The Impact of Objections in Nonjury Trials – Seldom Reversed
Many objections, especially to the forms of questions, seldom result
in reversals even in jury trials. And, it would be extremely rare for
an appellate court to reverse a nonjury trial decision based on an
objection to the form of a question or the form of an answer.
Although objection battles on the forms of questions do take place in
jury trials, such battles are less important in nonjury trials because
the judge is presumed to ignore inadmissible evidence and decide
the case only on evidence that was admissible.

**Common Phrases from Court Opinions Summarizing That
Inadmissible Evidence in A Nonjury Trial Will Not Result in A
Reversal Include:**
- "Trial judges often have access to inadmissible and highly
    prejudicial information and are presumed to be able to discount
    or disregard it."
 - "In bench trials, judges routinely hear inadmissible evidence that
    they are presumed to ignore."
- "The presumption that the trial judge disregarded all inadmissible
    evidence in reaching his decision."
- "It is presumed that improper evidence taken under objection was
    given no weight in reaching the final conclusion [in a nonjury
    trial] unless the contrary appears."
- "A judge, as factfinder, is presumed to disregard inadmissible
    evidence and consider only competent evidence."
- "A judge "must be presumed to be able to disregard inflammatory
    evidence"

Common Objections to the Form of the Question

Objections to the form of the question often have no clear answers or standards. Many judges and lawyers might disagree as to whether some question is improper or not. If a rule is cited when making the objection, it would usually be Rule 611.

Argumentative (also called **Harassing, Badgering**) **(R611)**
An argumentative question asks the witness to accept the examiner's summary, inference, or conclusion rather than a fact. Often the objector is trying to protect a witness during cross-examination.
Examples of Argumentative Questions:
"Isn't what you told this judge on its face ridiculous?"
"How can you expect the judge to believe that?"
"Are you telling this court that you don't know what a machete is?"
"Do you really expect the judge to believe that?"
"Do you mean to tell me...?"
"Doesn't it seem strange that...?"
"Your kind of the hatchet man down here for the D.A.s Office, aren't you?"
"It wouldn't bother you any, to come in here and lie from the time you started to the time you stopped, would it?"

Asked and Answered: This rule is violated by repeating the same question, asked by the same lawyer, to get the same answer, from the same witness, and is not permitted under R611. A question which has previously been asked and answered is being asked again. The rule prevents cumulative testimony R403. Repeating the testimony of a witness who has previously given the same testimony after being asked the same question by the same lawyer in not permitted. However, similar questions are often permitted if the identical information is not repeated. This objection does not apply to prevent the same questions being asked on cross-examination that were asked on direct examination. It does not prevent asking identical questions of different witnesses, nor does it prevent a lawyer representing a co-party from asking the same questions to the same witness again.

Assuming Facts Not in Evidence. This rule is violated when part of a question (usually the first part) assumes the truth of a fact that is in dispute but has not yet been proved at trial. Such a question is unfair because it cannot be answered without conceding the unproven fact. Assuming facts not in evidence may be an attempt to bring into the trial information that the lawyer is not able to prove by other means. However, questions that assume facts are permitted on cross-examination to impeach a witness's credibility.

Examples of assuming facts not in evidence:

> "When did you stop beating your wife?" (assumes previous beatings)
>
> "Did you know their business dropped 50% because of what the defendant did?" (assumes the defendant did the same thing)
>
> "How long after you purchased the items were they given to the defendant?" (assumes the purchase)

Responses:

"I will connect it up later."(Which just means, "Judge trust me and allow a few more questions." And, if you request permission to "connect up later" you'd better be able to connect it up or the judge will no longer trust you.)

> "I have a good faith basis for assuming those facts. I would like to proceed without further tipping my hand."
>
> "This is criminal case and the defendant has a Sixth Amendment right to fully cross-examine the witness."

Beyond the Scope (of a prior examination). Questions on redirect examination cannot go into subject matters that have not been covered in the previous cross-examination. Similarly, questions on re-cross examination cannot go beyond the scope of redirect examination. Redirect examination is limited to issues raised by the opposing lawyer on cross-examination. If the questions go beyond the issues raised on cross, the objection will be valid.

Responses.

> "Your Honor, I'm allowed to go into this area because it goes to the witness's credibility."

Note well: Cross-examination is not limited to the subjects covered on direct examination. If it were so limited, the cross examiner would be prohibited from fully examining the witness and exposing weaknesses in the direct exam. If a "beyond the scope" objection is raised to a cross-examination question, the best response probably would be, "Your Honor, R611 allows me to cross on the subject matter of direct examination and "matters affecting the witness's credibility." My cross goes to credibility."

Compound Question.

A compound question has two or more separate questions in a single question, and usually contains the words "and" or "or." A simple "yes" or "no" answer to the question will be unclear. If the witness asked answers "yes" or "no," it is not clear if the "yes" or "no" applies to all the multiple parts of the question or just one part.

Examples:

"On that day, you went shopping <u>and</u> to the beach, didn't you?"

"Did you determine the time of death by interviewing witnesses <u>and</u> by requesting the autopsy report?"

"On that Saturday, did you send the email <u>and</u> also call the banker?"

Cumulative (R403)

Cumulative questions ask for the same information from the same witness multiple times (like asked and answered) or ask multiple witnesses to establish the same facts.

Lack of Foundation (R901)

A lack of foundation objection arises when the lawyer asks a question before establishing the preliminary facts which would permit the questions. The evidence lacks testimony as to its authenticity or source.

Leading Question (R611)

A leading question improperly suggests the answer that the lawyer wants on direct examination. Another test is that the question contains the desired answer. The danger is that the question will make the witness agree with a false suggestion. Often leading questions start with phrases like - "Isn't it true that…" "Did…?" Or ends with "…,right?" Questions that start with the word "So" should be at least a yellow flag that the question might be leading. Although some questions are obviously leading, lawyers and judges often have very different interpretations of what a leading question is. Be prepared to quickly rephrase your question if an objection to it is sustained. Whether or not a question that contains the phrase "whether or not" is leading has been subject to much debate. A lawyer's nonverbal behavior or voice inflection is sometimes considered when determining whether a question is leading.

Leading questions are permissible for preliminary matters, when a party calls a hostile witness or an adverse witness (Rule 611) or when a witness is very young, very old, or mentally challenged. Leading questions are also common and proper on direct examination when laying foundations because under Rule 104 the rules of evidence do not apply, except for privileges, when asking preliminary questions about the admissibility of evidence. Leading questions are also permissible when they are used like a topic sentence in a paragraph to move a witness on direct examination to another part of the scene. For example," Did there come a time when you went into the store?" Of course, the lawyer could get the same result by simply making the statement, "Now I want to ask you some questions about what you did when you went into the store." It is a common belief that the more a lawyer leads on direct examination, the less credibility the witness will have because the witness looks like they are being told what to say during the examination.

Motion to strike

Motions to strike are used two ways. First, Rule of Civil Procedure 12(f) allows for motions to strike certain pleadings. Second, Motions to strike, under evidence R103, are treated similarly to objections and ask the judge to strike inadmissible testimony from the record if the witness has just said the objectionable words. Of course, "striking" is not really striking. The inadmissible words are not removed from the court records but remain in the record even if the testimony is "stricken." The opposing lawyer can ask the judge to instruct the jury to disregard the "stricken" testimony, but psychologically, such an instruction to "disregard" the testimony might highlight the testimony for the jury. Tough choices to make.

Narrative Question, or Calls for A Narrative Answer, or simply Narrative Answer

A narrative objection can refer to a question that asks a witness to tell a story rather than to state only a few specific facts, or refer to witness' answer which is several sentences, or even paragraphs, long. On one hand, narrative answers allow the witness to easily include inadmissible evidence, but on the other hand, a narrative story might more likely provide truthful facts.

Examples of narrative questions:
> "What did you do that day?"
> "Tell us about the accident."
> "Now tell us what everyone said and did at that point."
> "What happened that night?"
> "How did the accident happen?"
> Ans: "First thing I got up and I... Then I went to... After that I ... She told me that... And I immediately saw the ..."

Non-Responsive Answer: The non-responsive answer objection is made to an answer that does not answer the question that was asked. Simply, the witness does not answer the question asked by the lawyer. The witness is trying to make their own point and take control of the testimony. A problem with nonresponsive answers is that the witness is volunteering information that might be irrelevant or unfairly prejudicial. <u>In theory, only the lawyer asking the question can object to a non-responsive answer.</u> Some judges will only allow this objection from the lawyer who is asking the question. If the objection is sustained, it is often followed by a motion to strike the answer from the record. If the opposing lawyer is considering making a non-responsive answer objection, they are should consider some other appropriate objection such as "irrelevant," "unfairly prejudicial," or "lack of foundation."

Example of a non-responsive answers:
> Q: "Did you see the other driver get out of his car right after the accident?"
> A: "He told me he had insurance."
>
> Q: "Weren't you the last person the victim saw on the night of his death?"
> A: "I had nothing to do with that!"

Speculation – Calls for Speculation – Lack Person Knowledge. (R602)
A speculation objection is proper if the lawyer asks the witness a question that the witness has no personal knowledge about, or the witness testifies about something they have not perceived. A red flag signaling a call for speculation is often a question that starts with, Isn't it possible that…?" A better phrasing to accomplish the same objective would be to focus the question on the witness's personal knowledge and experience by asking for the same information but stating it as follows, "You don't know whether or not…, do you?"
Examples of a question calling for speculation:
 "What do you think he was thinking about at that time?"
"Why would she do something like that?"

Vague and Ambiguous Question: Vague and ambiguous questions are asked in ways that are incomprehensible, incomplete, or the answer will be ambiguous. If you, as the opposing lawyer, do not understand the question asked by your opponent, then the witness probably does not understand the question either. Object.

Other Objections

Golden Rule
The Golden Rule objection is made when the opposing counsel places the trier of fact (judge or jury) in the same situation that the case is about.
Examples of a Golden Rule objection:
 "Your Honor, what would you have done in a situation like that?"
 "Ladies and gentlemen of the jury, would you want someone like that coming into your neighborhood?"

Speaking Objections

A speaking objection is a lawyer's attempt to influence the jury by speaking to the jury by using the objection. Although such objections are very disfavored by judges in jury trials, in nonjury trials such objections can be used to make an argument to the trial judge and influence the decision to be made on the objection.

Examples of speaking objections:

"Well Judge, I am going to strongly object to this procedure. I feel that I am being sandbagged here and I don't appreciate it."

"Your honor, it doesn't matter what the answer is. Opposing counsel just wants to make a statement. He doesn't care what this witness says,"

Coaching the witness

Such objections can be used to communicate with and coach a witness.

Example of coaching the witness through an objection:

"Objection. The witness couldn't possibly know that answer."

Witness then responds by saying, "I don't know."

Relevance

Questions in a case about some other person, some other event, and some other time, are irrelevant unless the judge find such questions to be relevant in this particular case for a special reason such as to show bias or relevant in this case under Rule 404(b). I call such irrelevant evidence P.E.T. evidence and tell my students that PET evidence is not admissible - evidence about some other Person, or Event, or Time. Furthermore, questions about "**what most people do**" are almost always irrelevant.

Examples of irrelevant "what most people do" objections:

"Don't most people know that...?"

"Don't most people speed when their car is headed downhill?"

A Few Useful Definitions

Stipulation: Agreement between opposing lawyers to admit certain evidence without the normal in-court proof. The trier of fact then assumes the fact to have been proven.

Offer of Proof:
A statement by a lawyer describing E that the lawyer wants admitted. Proponent summarizes the substance of the excluded evidence to the judge to persuade the judge and to make a record for appeal. – R103

Motion in Limine:
A pre-trial motion seeking a ruling to admit or exclude evidence.

Limited Admissibility:
Evidence can be admitted for one purpose or against one party, but not admitted for another purpose or against another party. – R105

Intrinsic Impeachment - out of the witness' own mouth (almost always) on cross-examination. After a direct exam, the witness is impeached on cross. Almost always permissible.

Extrinsic Impeachment – impeachment coming for the testimony of another witness or the use of a document to impeach. If a witness is not impeached on cross by the opponent's questions, not all types of impeachment are permitted as extrinsic impeachment. The most common limitation is R608(b) – prior bad acts related to dishonestly.

Collateral - relevant only to discredit; does not go to a material matter.

A List of Common Possible Objections

Ambiguous	Improper opinion
Argumentative	Improper rehabilitation
Asked and answered	Inadmissible opinion
Assumes facts not in evidence	Incompetent witness
Authentication	Incomplete Inflammatory
Badgering	Insufficient foundation
Best evidence	Irrelevant (Relevance)
Beyond the scope	Lack of foundation
Bias	Lack of personal knowledge
Bolstering	Leading question
Calls for a conclusion	Misleading
Calls for speculation	Misquotes a witness or exhibit
Chain of custody	Misquotes evidence
Collateral	Misstates witness
Competence	More prejudicial than probative
Compound question	Motion to strike
Compromise / Settlement offer	Narrative
Confrontation (lack of)	(Question calls for a narrative)
Confusing	Narrative answer
Counsel is testifying	Non-responsive
Cumulative	Nothing pending
Document speaks for itself	Outside the scope of cross
Expert (Improper opinion)	Overly broad or general
Expert (not qualified)	Parole evidence rule
Habit	Personal knowledge
Harassing the witness	Prejudice (unfair)
Hearsay	Privilege communication
Hypothetical question misused	Relevance
Improper character evidence	Speculation/ Opinion/ Lack of
Improper characterization	personal knowledge
Improper impeachment	Unintelligible
	Vague

There are many more possible objections,
limited only by the lawyer's imagination.

Judges and the local legal culture in your jurisdiction may have
other rules or approaches to objections that are not touched on in
this handbook. Ask around and learn about them.

Evidentiary Foundations

Foundations - Predicates - Laying the Foundation

Foundations are questions asked by a lawyer to set the groundwork (the foundation) for admitting evidence at trial. The asking of these questions is often referred to as "**laying the foundation**" for the evidence. The word "**predicates,**" when used by trial lawyers, refers to a series of form or sample questions that a lawyer must ask to establish the facts, events, or conditions which are required by the rules of evidence or caselaw before presenting other evidence. Predicates are the questions that are asked when laying the foundation for other evidence. The evidentiary foundation is like the foundation for a building. It provides a solid basis for building up the structure of the case at trial. The necessary foundational questions are not always obvious by reading the rules of evidence.

Foundations may come from local legal culture ("That's the way we do things in this jurisdiction") or from a lawyer or judges prior experience ("That's the way I was taught to do it," or ("That's what I think works best,"), so that's what I am requiring you to do."

Evidentiary Foundations

Bare-Bones Foundations

The foundations provided in this handbook are designed to be brief, what I call "bare-bones foundations." A "bare-bones" foundation uses the minimum necessary questions to admit a piece of evidence or testimony and is less concerned about the "weight" of the evidence to be admitted. Bare-bones foundations are commonly used in non-jury trials. The judge, as trier of fact, should understand the elements of each foundation. On the other hand, what I call **"advocacy foundations"** are more common in jury trials where a jury of laypeople will make the important factual determinations in the case. An advocacy foundation uses much more than the bare minimum number of questions to lay the foundation, with additional questions going to enhance the persuasiveness of the sponsoring witness and the evidence. For example, when using a police officer's report to refresh memory, for recorded recollection, or to impeach, the additional questions might include questions relating to the training or conduct of the officer, such as:

"Did you have training in writing reports?"

"How much training?"

"When you are writing your report, you know that your supervisor will read some of your reports?"

"You know that your future assignments might depend on the quality of your written reports?"

"Do you normally reread your report before submitting it?"

"Do you check your report for accuracy before submitting it?"

Admissibility v. Weight

Foundations are sometimes necessary for evidence to be admissible. As such, they go to the issue of "admissibility," which is about "can" the evidence be included in the trial so that the trier of fact (judge or jury) can consider that evidence in decision-making. On the other hand, the "weight" of evidence is the "value" to be given to the piece of evidence by the trier of fact. Trial judgments are usually determined by which party's admitted evidence is more persuasive, and has the party met the burden of persuasion to the necessary standard (such as: "preponderance of the evidence" or "beyond a reasonable doubt").

Example of Admissibility and Weight

Assume the trial is about a fight. One person says, "He hit me." The other person says, "I did not." Both statements will be admissible, but the trier of fact, after listening to other facts and witnesses, will probably assign different weights or values to the testimony of the two people. Typically, one person will be considered more credible or believable than the other person. The more reliable person's testimony it is said to be given greater weight. It is that weight of the evidence that will eventually lead to a decision for one party or the other. A common statement made by a judge when an opposing party argues against the admissibility of testimony or other evidence is, "That goes to weight, not admissibility." Such a statement by a judge means, "You just lost your battle to exclude that evidence from the trial, but you can still argue that your case is stronger and more persuasive than your opponent's case is."

3 Simple Questions

After handing a physical item to a witness and saying for the record, "Let me show you what has been marked as proposed exhibit number one," the foundation for some physical pieces of evidence can be established with as few as three questions:

---

1) **Q: What is it?**

2) **Q: How do you know that?**

3) **Q: Is it in the same condition as it was on the day of ...?"**
   (Or, "Is that a fair and accurate representation of the item as it was on ...?").

Steps for Introducing Exhibits

Preliminary steps are:
1) Have the exhibit marked for identification
2) Show the proposed exhibit to opposing counsel
3) Ask permission to approach the witness with the proposed exhibit

---

1. History - How the witness knows the exhibit.

Offer some testimony that the witness <u>knows</u> or is <u>familiar with</u> the evidence – such as a document, physical item, photo, diagram, scene, text message, email - or recalls the statement. Even if the witness has only seen the exhibit once before or has just been to the scene shown in the photograph once before, <u>once is enough</u>.

2. The Litany (a ritualistic repetition of foundational questions)

a) Ask the court clerk to **mark the item** (using numbers or letters). The clerk will decide which system to use. In more serious cases in the jurisdiction's higher courts (typically where jury trials are allowed), exhibits are usually required to be marked at least before trial starts, and often during pretrial conferences.

b) **Show opposing counsel** (this will prevent interruptions) and say, "Let the record reflect that I am showing the defense what has been marked as plaintiff's proposed exhibit number one."

c) Ask the judge for **permission to approach** the witness. "May I approach the witness?"

- Q: "**I show you what has been marked as** Plaintiff's (Prosecution's) (Defense's) proposed exhibit # x (or exhibit #x for identification purposes) **and ask whether you can identify it**" (You expect a "yes" answer here.)

- Q: "**What is it?**" (They describe it in general terms. "It is the contract/photo of the scene/weapon recovered/drugs seized/diagram of the area/etc.")

- Q: "**How do you know that?**" (They answer – "I recognize it. It has my signature on it. / I have been there many times before. / I put my initials on it and the defendant's name/etc.")

3. Show Condition or Comparison or Accuracy

Some comparison must be made between the exhibit in court and when the witness became familiar with the exhibit out-of-court. Of the examples that follow, only one such question is necessary.

- "Is this in the **same** condition as when you... [first saw it...seized it...etc.]?"
- "Is this in the **same or substantially the same condition**.... as when you..."   (for item or document)
- "Is it a **fair and accurate representation** of the ... **as it was that day**?"   (for diagram or pictures)
- "**Has it changed** in any significant way?"
- "**How does it compare** to the item you saw that day?"

4. Move or Offer the Exhibit into Evidence

"Your honor, **I offer the exhibit into evidence**." - or, "I move the exhibit into evidence."

You could instead say, "I offer proposed exhibit # 1 into evidence as exhibit # 1," but why make it so confusing? Just say, "I offer the exhibit into evidence."

The judge <u>might</u> ask the opposing counsel, "Any objections?" but the opponent should object immediately after the proponent offers the exhibit, if there is an objection to the admissibility (not the weight). The judge should allow "voir dire" (immediate cross examination limited to the foundation and the admissibility) by the opponent of the exhibit.

The Common Evidentiary Foundations

Physical Items
Photograph (printed)
Diagram of scene
Physical item seized at scene

Common Documents
Refreshing memory
Recorded recollection
Business records in paper
Business records – and self-authentication under R902
Deposition Impeachment (see below)

Records and Treatises
Public record
Learned treatise –
> Use on direct supporting your expert
> Use on cross attacking their expert

Digital Evidence – from the internet, a cell phone, or a computer
Also called - ESI – Electronically Stored Information
Emails
Text message – issues of incompleteness
Social Media - Facebook, Instagram, Twitter, Snapchat
Website posting
Voicemail recording
Videos, including on cell phone
Photo on cell phone
Fax
Chatroom conversations

Impeachment
> Impeaching by Prior Written Inconsistent statement
> Impeaching by Omission in Prior Written Statement
> Impeaching by Prior Oral Inconsistent statement
> Impeaching by Inconsistent Oral Deposition Transcript

Phrases to Move Evidence into a Trial

(Pick one and always use it)

"I offer the exhibit into evidence." (By far the easiest to use)

"Your Honor, I ask that what's been previously marked as Plaintiff's Exhibit A for Identification be admitted into evidence as Plaintiff's A."

"At this time, we offer Plaintiff's A for identification into evidence as Plaintiff's exhibit A."

"The Government at this time, would move to introduce Government's Exhibit No. 2 into evidence."

"Your Honor, we'd offer Defense Exhibit B into evidence."

"Your Honor, I move that Plaintiff's Exhibit 3 be introduced into evidence."

"We offer Exhibit A into evidence."

"Your honor, I would like to submit People's exhibit 'A' into evidence."

"We would ask the Court to admit State's Exhibit 4 for Identification as State's 4."

Useful Points to Remember

Offering something "into evidence" means that in a jury trial the exhibit can go into the jury room and be reviewed as many times as the jurors want to look at it.

Make an Offer of Proof – if your evidence is not admitted. R103.

Hearsay within hearsay – statements incorporated into other statements need an additional hearsay exception to be admissible. R805 Hearsay Within Hearsay.

Public records do not have to be "open to the public" but rather are reports and records created by public (government) employees. R803(8)

A record automatically generated by a computer - is not hearsay (computer generated records). No assertion by a person.

Email offered to show notice, knowledge, or fear are not assertions and therefore not hearsay. In a contract or consent form, the words have independent legal significance, which means they operate to form a contract even if they are not true.

Demonstrative evidence – demonstrates or represents some real evidence. Also sometimes called **illustrative evidence**, as compared to **real evidence**, which as some historical connection to the case - such as being the drugs, the gun, etc.

A "chain of custody" is required for fungible items that cannot be identified and distinguished on sight, such as drugs, alcohol, and blood examples - indistinguishable as grains of sand. Often, they are taken into custody and forwarded for laboratory testing. The "chain" makes sure the evidence that is tested is connected to the correct case.

Distinctive characteristics Evidence tags with initials and case names make items unique and should qualify as a **"Distinctive characteristic"** under R901(b)(4) for authentication purposes.

The most common method to introduce physical and documentary evidence is **using personal knowledge and distinctive characteristics.** R901(b)(1)&(4)

Affidavits are hearsay and not admissible at trial. However, affidavits can be used in summary judgment proceedings if the statements in the affidavits would be admissible in court if testified to by the declarant with personal knowledge. Therefore, lawyers should not be signing affidavits for summary judgement. Potential witnesses with personal knowledge of the facts must sign the affidavits.

HARROWing - a Barkai acronym formed from the first letters of evidence concepts most likely to impact admissibility decisions. Always think of HARROWing when a physical item is going to be introduced, especially if the item is a document or a physical item with words on it. **H**earsay R800s, **A**uthentication R900s, **R**elevance R401, **R**elevance R403, **O**riginal **W**ritings (Best Evidence) R1000s. HARROWing applies to ESI (Electronically Stored Information) such as emails, texts, websites, etc.

OTP - what is the evidence "Offered to Prove?" OTP impacts relevance, admissibility, and the necessary foundation.

The rules of evidence do not tell you how to introduce exhibits although some rules do list the foundational elements which must be included in foundational questions. The hearsay exceptions of Recorded Recollection R803(5) and Records of a Regular Conducted Activity (business records) R803(6) are examples of hearsay exceptions that are so complicated that a novice trial lawyer might want to have the rule in front of them when attempting to lay the foundation.

Laying a foundation is like a sport. Practice before the game.

Steps: Mark/Pre-Mark, Show, Approach, Foundational Questions, Offer
> **Mark exhibits**: 1 day before trial or prior to trial – depending on the court rules.

Magic Words: "**in the same or substantially the same condition**" or "**fair and accurate representation**," or "**fairly accurate representation**," or "**fairly represent**."

Speak in generic terms when talking about exhibits until the witness identifies the exhibit: "Proposed exhibit # 1" or "Exhibit # 1 for identification purposes," not "Your report," or "Photo of the scene."

To "publish" an exhibit means to show the exhibit to the jury or ask the judge to look at the exhibit now.

Chain of evidence is usually only necessary for fungible items (identical - they all look the same), or items that need testing – drugs, alcohol, blood, DNA. Not every "kink in the link" of the chain of evidence makes evidence inadmissible. Authentication only requires production of evidence "sufficient to support a finding," R901(a)(1), which is a low standard.

Basic tasks that every trial lawyer should be able to do
- introduce documents, physical items, photographs
- refresh memory (almost always done on direct)
- use the recollection recorded hearsay exception (almost always done on direct).
- impeach (almost always done on cross); inconsistent statements & omissions.

The Best Foundation Resources
- Grimm, Joseph & Capra, Best Practices for Authenticating Digital Evidence 69 Baylor L.R. 1 (2017)
- Evidentiary Foundations for Government Attorneys (2015) (from National Attorneys General Training & Research Institute) - (JB: It contains many simple foundations.)
- Edward Imwinkelried, Evidentiary Foundations, (10th ed. 2018) – (The classic source for foundations, but less than you might want about ESI foundations, and more than you might want in the middle of trial.)
- Deanne Siemer, Laying Foundations and Meeting Objections (4th ed. 2013)

Important Evidence Rules to Guide You

R103(c) Directing an Offer of Proof. – explains how to protect your record if your evidence is excluded.

R104 Preliminary questions.
(a) In General. In [deciding preliminary questions] the court is <u>not</u> <u>bound by evidence rules</u> except those on privilege. **JB:** meaning <u>you</u> <u>can lead on direct for foundations.</u>]
(b) Relevance that Depends on a Fact. When the relevance of evidence depends on whether a fact exists, proof must be introduced <u>sufficient to support a finding</u> that the fact does exist.
[**JB**: <u>that is a low threshold.</u>]

R901 Authenticating or Identifying Evidence.
(a) In General. To satisfy the requirement of authenticating or identifying an item of evidence, the proponent must produce <u>evidence sufficient to support a finding</u> that the item is what the proponent claims it is. [**JB**: <u>that is a low threshold</u>]
(b) Examples. The following are examples only —
    (1) Testimony of a Witness with Knowledge. Testimony that an item is what it is claimed to be.
    (4) Distinctive Characteristics and the Like. The appearance, contents, substance, internal patterns, or other <u>distinctive</u> <u>characteristics</u> of the item, <u>taken together with all the</u> <u>circumstances.</u>
    (7) Evidence About Public Records.
    (9) Evidence About a Process or System.

R612 Writing Used to Refresh a Witness's Memory. Witness does not need to be the author. Anything can be used to refresh memory - even "my left shoe" – My in-class example.

R613 Witness's Prior Statement. Impeachment by inconsistent statements and omissions.

R801(d)(1) Not Hearsay: A Declarant-Witness's Prior Statement. (Inconsistent under oath, consistent, or prior ID)

R803(6) Records of a Regularly Conducted Activity
(JB: <u>business records are</u> **KRAP)**
    (**K**ept in the course, **R**egular practice, **A**t or near the time, **P**ersonal knowledge)

R902 Evidence That Is Self-Authenticating

902(11) Certified Domestic Records of a Regularly Conducted Activity. [Note: There are many certification forms available on the internet.]

902(13) Certified Records Generated by an Electronic Process or System.

902(14) Certified Data Copied from an Electronic Device, Storage Medium, or File.

R105 Limited Admissibility (admitted against only one party or for a limited purpose)

R106 Remainder of / related writing [JB: admit now]

R1006 Summaries...voluminous writings which cannot conveniently be examined in court.

**The Opponent Has the Burden
On the Issue of Trustworthiness of Records**

Burden of showing a record lacks trustworthiness is on the opponent in the Federal rules - R803(6)(7)(8) ..."and, the opponent does not show ...a lack of trustworthiness."

Basic Foundations & Impeachment Examples

Several of the following foundation and impeachment examples are based upon the facts of

Nita Liquor Commission v. Cut-Rate Liquor and Jones*

In this famous, fictional case from NITA (National Institute of Trial Advocacy), Walter Watkins was observed going into the Cut-Rate Liquor Store by Officer Bier and his partner from their unmarked car which was parked across the street from the liquor store. The officers had a partial view into the store and saw Watkins appear to purchase liquor at the counter. Watkins was arrested outside the store as he was leaving with a brown paper bag which contained a bottle of Thunderbird Wine. Cut-Rate Liquors and the clerk Dan Jones were issued citations for selling liquor to a person under the influence of liquor.

* This NITA Liquor Problem is used with the permission of the National Institute of Trial Advocacy (NITA). The terms "Officer Bier, Thunderbird Wine, Jackson & 7th Street, April 5th, Walter Watkins, and shoulders up" used in this publication are original to the Nita Liquor Commission v. Cut-Rate Liquor and Jones problem from *Problems in Trial Advocacy* by Donald H. Beskind and Anthony J. Bocchino, published by the National Institute of Trial Advocacy. The basis of the NITA Liquor problem and the specified terms are used here with permission.

NITA Liquor Commission
v.
Jones

The Facts

This case is a civil action brought by the Liquor Commission against Dan Jones and the Cut-Rate Liquor Store, for civil penalties, including possible revocation of Cut-Rate's liquor license. Investigator Bier is a typical investigator-police officer and has investigated many such incidents. Bier's official report appears on the next page along with a diagram of the scene.

Dan Jones and the Cut-Rate Liquor Store deny that Watkins was intoxicated on the evening of April 5 when he was in their store. Jones says that Watkins did not appear to be intoxicated when he observed Watkins in the store. Watkins was convicted of public intoxication at a prior trial. Watkins is not present for this Cut-Rate case.

1. Prepare to do a direct examination of Officer Bier for the government.

2. Prepare to do a cross examination of Officer Bier for the Defense.

Officer Bier's Report

NITA LIQUOR COMMISSION OFFICIAL REPORT

My partner Donald Smith and I are investigators for the Nita Liquor Commission. On the evening of April 5, at approximately 8:45 p.m., we were parked near the Cut-Rate Liquor Store when we observed an individual, later identified as Walter Watkins, attempting to cross 7th Street. Mr. Watkins was staggering and had great difficulty making it to the other side of the street. He stumbled and almost fell at the curb on the south side of 7th Street. He walked to the entrance of the Cut-Rate Liquor Store, and then paused for a few moments before he entered the store. The front of the store had a plate glass window with displays and advertising in it. From our car, we could see Mr. Watkins from the shoulders up through the window. We observed Mr. Watkins approach the counter and say a few words to the clerk, Dan Jones. A few minutes later, Watkins emerged from the store carrying a bottle of Thunderbird wine in a brown paper sack.

I stopped Mr. Watkins as he exited the store. I detected the odor of alcohol and administered a field sobriety test. I then arrested Watkins and issued him a citation for public intoxication, seized the wine, and issued a citation to Dan Jones and the Cut-Rate Liquor store for violation of H.R.S. 281-78 which contains the following language:

> No licensee nor its employees shall sell or furnish any liquor to any person at the time under the influence of liquor.

I have attached a diagram of the scene to this report.

Date: April 5   Time: 22:15

signed J. Bier

_____

Diagram of Cut-Rate Liquor Store Area

A- Cut-Rate Liquor Store
B- Plate Glass Windows
C- Cash Register
D- Officers Vehicle
E- Watkins Arrested

Photograph of a Scene

Introduce a photograph of Cut-Rate Liquor Store where the clerk and the liquor store were charged with selling liquor to an intoxicated person. R901(B)(1) (Testimony of a Witness with Knowledge)

Q: Officer Bier, where were you on the night of April 5?
A: Parked in an unmark car outside Cut-Rate Liquor Store.

Q: Let me show you what has been marked as Plaintiff's proposed exhibit # 1.   What is it?
A: It is a photograph of Cut-Rate Liquor Store where I was parked on April 5th.

Q: How do you know that?
A: I was at the store that night. I recognize it. I took the photo.

Q: Is the photograph a fair and accurate representation of Cut-Rate Liquor store as it appeared on April 5th?
A: Yes.

Q: Your Honor, I offer the exhibit into evidence.

Enhancements/Additional Questions
- "Please describe the appearance of the store."
- "How many times have you seen the Cut-Rate Liquor Store?" (Ask this question only if the witness has been to the store many times. However, being there once is enough for the foundation.) The witness can authenticate the photo even if the trial event was the only time the witness ever saw the store pictured in the photo

Additional Points:
- The photographer is not a necessary witness.
- The witness's personal knowledge of the contents of the photograph is all that is necessary.
- The witness does not have to have seen the photograph before coming to court.
- Print the photo and bring copies to court for the judge, jury, and opposing counsel.
- The photo could be a "Street view" from Google Maps that the witness has never seen before.

Diagram of the Scene

Demonstrative Evidence

Diagram from Officer Bier's Report

After some testimony about the events.

Q: Officer Bier, did you make a diagram of the scene that night? (Ans: Yes)

Q: Let me show you what has been marked as Plaintiff's proposed exhibit # 1. <u>What is it?</u> (Ans: My diagram)

Q: <u>How do you know that?</u> (Ans: I drew it. I remember it. That's my writing)

Q: Is it a <u>fair and accurate representation</u> of the intersection of Jackson and 7th Streets <u>on April 5th</u>? (Ans: Yes.)

Q: Is the proposed exhibit in the <u>same condition</u> as it was when you drew it on April 5th? (Ans: Yes.)

Q: Your Honor, I offer the exhibit into evidence.

Real Evidence

The Bottle of Thunderbird Wine Seized by Officer Bier

After some testimony about the events.

Q: Officer Bier, <u>what, if anything, did you recover</u> from Mr.
        Watkins that night?
        (Ans: A bottle and a bag)

Q: Let me hand you what has been marked as Plaintiff's proposed
        exhibit # 2. <u>What is it?</u>
        (Ans: The bottle and bag I seized from Watkins)

        [If the bottle is in a bag, leave it in the bag. Have both the bottle
        and bag marked separately, e.g., Exhibits 1 and 2, A and B, 1
        and 1A. Let the witness take the bottle out of the bag, like
        unwrapping a present. It will create some interest in what might
        be an otherwise boring trial.]

Q: <u>How do you know that?</u>
        [Ans: My initials, in my handwriting, are on the bag along with
        the words "Cut-Rate Liquor" and "April 5."]

Q: Is the proposed exhibit # 2 <u>in the same or substantially the same
        condition</u> as it was when you recovered it from Watkins on
        April 5th?
        (Ans: Generally, yes. However, some of the liquid was removed
        for testing for alcohol.)

Q: Your Honor, I offer the exhibit into evidence.

Offering A Contract into Evidence

Q: Mr. Johnny, I now want to ask you some questions about your dealings with Mr. King. In September, two years ago, did you have several conversations with Mr. King?

A: Yes. I did.

Q: What was the result of those conversations?

A: Mr. King and I entered into a contract for legal work.

Assume the exhibit has been pre-marked before the day of trial

Q: Let the record reflect that I am handing Mr. Johnny what has been pre-marked, as required by Court Rule, Plaintiff's proposed Exhibit # 1.
What is it Mr. Johnny?

A: It's the contract between me and Mr. King for the legal work that I was going to do for him.

Q: How do you know that? [Prepare the witness to answer this question]

A: I drafted this contract. I recognize it. That's my signature on it as well as Mr. King's.

Q: Is the contract in the same condition as it was two years when you both signed it.

A: Yes. There are no alterations to the contract.

Q: You Honor, I offer the exhibit into evidence

Refreshing Memory
(Anything can be used to refresh memory)

Refreshing memory is almost always done on direct examination. Impeachment is almost always done on cross examination.

In the NITA case, assume witness Bier forgets some of Mr. Watkin's movements on the street. Refresh Bier's memory from his report. R612.

Q: Please describe Watkin's movements as he crossed 7th Street.
A: He staggered and had great difficulty getting to the other side of the street.

Q: Do you recall anything else about Watkins as he crossed the street.
A: Not really

Q: Officer Bier did you make a report in this case? A: Yes.

Q: Let me hand you what has been marked as Plaintiff's proposed exhibit # 3. What is it?
[Note: You are not going to introduce the document. Some judges might allow you to refresh memory without marking the exhibit, but the better practice is to have the document marked.]
A: My report.

Q: Please read it to yourself, especially the 4th and 5th lines.
(Note: You can focus the witness on what you want to witness to pay attention to.)

Q: Let the record reflect that I am taking proposed exhibit # 3 away from the Officer.
Now Officer Bier, is your memory refreshed?
A: Yes.

Q: What else do you now recall about how Watkins crossed 7th Street?
A: Watkins stumbled as he crossed 7th Street
(Discussion continued on the next page)

Recommendation: I suggest that you do not ask the witness, "Would anything refresh your memory." Just start refreshing. Isn't it strange to say, "Witness, I know you cannot remember, but can you remember anything that would help you remember what you have already forgotten?" Just refresh.

Additional points: The document used to refresh is not introduced into evidence. The witness' memory was refreshed. There is no need to introduce the document. There is no hearsay issue.

Writing Used to Refresh Memory

If a writing was used to refresh memory, R612 allows

as a matter of right, if the document was used in court;
with judge's discretion, if the document was used out of court

the opponent to:

1) see the writing in court,
2) inspect it
3) cross-examine on it, and
4) introduce portions of it (related to the testimony)

Simply: **Get, Inspect, Cross, Introduce.**

However, it would be very unusual for an opponent to introduce the document because most of the document would hurt the opponent's case. If the opponent wanted to introduce only portions of the document, the lawyer who used it to refresh memory would have an argument that under R106, in fairness other parts of the document should be considered at the same time.

Rule 612. Writing used to refresh memory. (paraphrased)
   If a witness uses a writing to refresh memory for the purpose of testifying, either:
   (1) while testifying; or
   (2) before testifying, if the court in its discretion determines it is necessary in the interests of justice,
      an adverse party is entitled
      to have the writing produced at the hearing,
      to inspect it,
      to cross-examine the witness thereon, and
      to introduce in evidence those portions which relate to the
         testimony of the witness.

Refreshing Memory with a Leading Question

(Using the same facts as the previous example)

Q: Do you recall anything else about Watkins as he crossed the street.

A: Not really

Q: Did he stumble and almost fall?

Opposing Lawyer: Objection: Leading

Q: I'll rephrase my question. What else do you recall about Watkins as he crossed the street.

A: Now I recall that he did stumble and almost fell crossing the street. I'm nervous. I forgot.

Note: The witness's credibility might have decreased somewhat because of the leading question, but the lawyer got the answer that was needed. The less important the information, the more likely leading will have little or no impact on your case.

Leading on Minor Issues When the Witness Has Gone Off Course

Q: What day of the week did this happen?

A: Tuesday.

Q: You said Tuesday. Did you actually mean Monday?

A: Oh right, sorry. It was Monday.

Recorded Recollection (Author's Rule)

Recorded recollection is a hearsay exception that allows <u>for reading into evidence</u> a statement that was made by a witness on the stand who can no longer recall the facts even after there has been attempts to refresh the witness's memory. Recorded recollection is <u>almost always done on direct examination</u> with a witness the lawyer has called to testify. This foundation is complicated and not intuitive.

In the NITA problem, assume that attempts to refresh the witness's memory did not work. Therefore, assume the previous question and answer were:

Q: What else do you now recall?
A: Sorry, I truly do not remember any more.

[Lawyer now moves into the foundation for Recorded Recollection, under R803(5).

Q: Let me again show you proposed exhibit # 3. That is your report of this incident, right? (Note: Leading is appropriate when establishing any foundations under FRE 103(a)).
A: Yes

Q: You made that report when the incident was <u>fresh</u> in your mind?
A: Yes, just about an hour after the incident.

Q: Does the report <u>accurately reflect your knowledge</u> of the incident at the time of the incident?
A: Yes.

Q: Although you <u>once knew the details</u> of the incident and wrote them in your report, right now <u>you cannot now recall</u> the details of the incident well enough <u>to testify fully and accurately</u>, right?
A: Yes.

Q: Your honor, I would now <u>like to read</u> into the record those parts of the report that the witness no longer remembers. [Or, you could ask to have the witness read the portions of the report.]

(Discussion continued on the next page)

RULE 803(5) Recorded Recollection A record that:

(A) is on a matter the witness once knew about but now cannot recall well enough to testify fully and accurately;

(B) was made or adopted by the witness when the matter was fresh in the witness's memory; and

(C) accurately reflects the witness's knowledge.

If admitted, the record may be read into evidence but may be received as an exhibit only if offered by an adverse party.

Additional Points: "Admission" into evidence comes from reading parts of the document into evidence. The document is not physically admitted by the proponent of the evidence. It cannot be taken into the jury room. Information in this hearsay document is admitted (heard) only once like oral testimony. Also, admitting information from a "Learned Treatise" under that hearsay exception R803(18) is a similar process in that the information from the treatise can only be read and not physically introduced.

Almost always, the witness was the author of the document used as the recorded recollection. Refreshing memory under R612 and recorded recollection are almost always done on direct examination. Witnesses are impeached on cross, not refreshed. You would not normally use recorded recollection on cross because almost all of the document goes against your client.

I think most lawyers prefer to read the recollection on direct examination themselves and not have the witness do it. By reading the recollection yourself, you can add what you consider the best tone, volume, pace, and emphasis for your case. Remember, when you use a past recollection recorded with your witness on direct, you cannot physically introduce the document into evidence. The proponent of the past recollection recorded "admits" the recollection by reading it, not physically admitting it.

Recorded recollection documents are not business records. Business records do get admitted into evidence. The difference is that if admitted, the evidence can be taken into the jury room and be consulted by the jury many times during deliberations.

A past recollection recorded includes all notes that a witness makes on any type of document. In evidence class, I pull out my wallet and show students all the recorded recollections that I have in my wallet (post-it notes, notes on business cards, notes on little scraps of paper, etc.) and any notes I have taken on my cell phone. Recorded Recollections and Statements in Learned Treatises, R803(18), are two types of hearsay documents which can only be read into evidence but not physically introduced, at least not by the proponent of a recorded recollection.

Business Records - Custodian of Records
(The actual hearsay exception is for
"Regularly Conducted Activity,"
but is usually called "Business Records")

To prove that Cut-Rate Liquors had Thunderbird Wine in stock on April 5, a business record can be offered.

Q: Please state your name, occupation, and why you are here today.

A: I am Mr. Data, an employee of Cut-Rate Liquors. My duties at Cut-Rate include serving as the custodian of business inventory records for Cut-rate. I am here today pursuant to a subpoena to bring inventory records of Cut-Rate for April 5th.

Q: Did you bring with you today a copy of the Cut-Rate inventory records pertaining to Thunderbird wine for April 5th with you?

A: Yes.

Q: Do you know how Cut-Rate maintains its inventory records?

A: Yes.

Q: I show you what has been pre-marked as proposed exhibit # 1 and ask if you can identify what it is?

A: Yes, I can. Those are the Cute-Rate inventory records that I brought to court.

Q: Are those inventory records made by a person with <u>personal knowledge,</u> <u>at or near the time</u> the inventory is taken?

A: Yes.

Q: Are those records <u>kept in the course of a regularly conducted activity</u> of a business?

A: Yes.

Q: Is making those records a <u>regular practice</u> of Cut-Rate's business?

A: Yes.

Q: Your Honor, I offer the exhibit into evidence.

Publishing a Business Record: After being admitted, the business record can be "published" (which means it can be shown to the trier to fact). Depending on the judge's practice, the lawyer might be able to have the information from the record read to jury when it is admitted. If so, the Q & A could be:

Q: What do those records say about whether Cut-Rate had Thunderbird Wine in stock on April 5th?

A: "Thunderbird Wine, quantity 5," which means that Cut-Rate had five bottles of Thunderbird Wine in stock on April 5.

Remember, **business records are KRAP**. That acronym always gets my students' attention, and it helps them remember the foundation's components. **KRAP** – means:
Kept in the course,
Regular practice,
At or near the time,
Personal knowledge

The **custodian of records or other qualified witness** required by the business record evidence rule is often the owner of the business, a bookkeeper, or anybody who works in the business. They just have to be able to answer questions to provide the appropriate foundation.

Although it adds to the weight of the evidence to have a witness who has been employed for many years in the data collection of the business, that is not required. The custodian only needs to be able to testify to the foundation requirements. The custodian could have only been the custodian for one day, if they can credibly answer the foundational questions (although that fact might go to the weight of the evidence, but not its admissibility). The custodian does not have to be employed on the day the record was made.

I would prefer to use a self-authenticating business record. The custodian is open to a difficult cross.
"Do you know who made the business entry?" – Know their work history? Have they been disciplined? Know their accuracy? Are they still with the company? (Of course, you need a good faith basis).

Self-Authenticating Business Records

The Federal Rules of Evidence were amended in 2002 to allow business records to be self-authenticated by a written certification of the custodian or other qualified witness, which means that a witness does not have to appear in court. R902(11)(12). Many states have created statutes or forms to be used for the certification. An example of such a certification affidavit follows and many are available on the internet.

TEXAS FORM

	Business Records Affidavit	
FORM AR-1(08/10)	Tax Year	HCAD Account Number

This affidavit should be executed before a Notary Public or other official authorized to administer oaths and attached to the applicable business records. Please print or type.

Before me, the undersigned authority, personally appeared _____, who being by me duly sworn, deposed as follows:

My name is _____, I am of sound mind, capable of making this affidavit, and personally acquainted with the facts herein stated:

I am the custodian of the records of _____. Attached hereto are
_____ pages of records from _____ . These
(NAME OF BUSINESS)
said _____ pages of records are kept by _____
(NAME OF BUSINESS)
in the regular course of business, and it was the regular practice of said entity for an employee or representative with knowledge of the act, event, condition, opinion, or diagnosis, recorded to make the record or to transmit information thereof to be included in such record; and the record was made at or near the time or reasonably soon thereafter. The records attached hereto are the original or exact duplicates of the original.

_____
Affiant's Signature

SWORN TO AND SUBSCRIBED before me on the _____ day of _____, _____

_____
Notary Public, State of Texas

(seal)   _____
Notary's Printed Name

_____
My commission expires

Demonstrative Evidence Similar to the Real Item

Assume the bottle of Thunderbird wine in the Nita Liquor Commission case was dropped and broken after the contents had been tested in the lab and showed that it contained alcohol. At trial, a lawyer wants to introduce a bottle similar to the actual bottle of Thunderbird wine.

Q: Officer Bier, do you recognize proposed exhibit # 5?
A: Yes. I do.

Q: What is it?
A: It is a bottle like the one sold by Cut-Rate on the night of the incident.

Q: How do you know that?
A: I am a Liquor Commission Investigator. I am very familiar with Thunderbird wine as part of my job.

Q: "Is this bottle similar to the bottle you seized from Watkins on April 5?"
A: Yes.

Q: I offer the exhibit into evidence.

If there is a relevance objection to the "similar" bottle, the lawyer examining the witness needs to be ready to say, "Your honor, this bottle is relevant to show ...[some appropriate statement]." For example, the size and weight of the bottle suggests that Mr. Watkins could not have smuggled the bottle into the liquor store under his clothing. The similar bottle is not offered as the bottle that was sold that night, but it is being offered to prove something else, which is an example of limited admissibility under R105. The lawyer should not say, although it might be true, "My evidence professor always told us to introduce some physical evidence into the trial to wake up the trier of fact." [Such a statement offers a good trial strategy, but not a good response to the judge's question about relevance.]

Impeachment by Prior Written Inconsistent Statement
R613

Impeach Officer Bier from his report in the NITA problem, assuming Bier testified on direct exam, "I saw Watkins from the waist up inside the store."

Direct exam testimony was "...from the <u>waist</u> up...."
Report says "...from the <u>shoulders</u> up..."

Q: <u>Today</u> you testified on direct examination[1] that you could see Watkins inside the store from the <u>waist up</u>? (said in a disbelieving tone) (Commit to today's testimony.)
A: Yes.

Q: You made a written report in this case within a few hours of the incident? (Credit prior statement's reliability)
A: Yes.

Q: Let the record reflect that I am handing the witness proposed exhibit #x. Mr. Bier, proposed exhibit #x is the report you made within a couple of hours after the incident?
A: Yes.

Q: That is your signature on the report?
A: Yes

Q: Even though you said on direct examination that you could see Mr. Watkins inside the store from the waist up, doesn't it say right here in your report (pointing to it) that "we could see Mr. Watkins from the <u>shoulders up</u> through the window"?
A: Yes.

(Discussion continued on the next page)

---

[1] I suggest that you only use the phrase – "You testified on direct" – when you are going to impeach a witness with a prior statement. Do not use that phrase when you are asking questions about a real event that took place in your case. What happened on the day of the incident might be different that what a witness testified to on direct. You should keep the trier of fact's attention on the incident itself, not the testimony on direct – unless you are impeaching that direct testimony.

Stop. Ask no further questions on this topic. Don't say, "Are you lying today or were you lying then?" Such a question is probably argumentative and objectionable anyway. Do not argue with the witness or ask the witness to admit they are not telling the truth. Save the credibility argument for closing argument. In closing argument, you can make an argument without having the witness trying to explain away your impeachment.

Understand the difference between testimony about "waist up" and "shoulders up." If Officer Bier could see Mr. Watkins inside the store from the waist up, he could have seen the bottle of wine, the cash register, any money changing hands, and the wine bottle changing hands. All those facts go to showing that there was a sale of wine in violation of the statute. However, if the officer could only see inside the store at the shoulders up level, then he was not able to see any direct sale and the defense has a better argument.

Three impeaching steps here: commit; credit; and confront. 1) <u>Commit</u> the witness to the statement made on direct, 2) <u>credit</u> the prior out-of-court statement, and 3) <u>confront</u> the witness with the difference.

<u>By putting the conflicting statements in one sentence by using a dependent clause</u> ("Even though you said on direct examination that…"), <u>the trier of fact cannot miss the contradiction.</u> Some impeaching lawyers will emphasize certain words in their questions, so the trier of fact does not miss the inconsistency. For example, they would emphasize with tone, volume, pace, and any other nonverbal's, the words "waist up" and "shoulder up." The impeaching lawyer might want to make eye contact with the judge or the jury when emphasizing those words.

Additional questions that are sometimes asked, especially if it is a jury trial:

> Your prior statement was made closer in time to the event than your statement today?
> Your memory was better at the earlier time?
> You have had training on how to write reports?
> You know that your supervisor will read your reports?
> You know that you are evaluated on, and perhaps even promoted or demoted based on the quality of your reports?

Impeachment by Omission

Assume that <u>Bier testified on direct exam,</u> "As I was sitting in my car watching Watkins <u>inside the store, I saw that Watkins stumble</u> <u>and almost fall as he approached the counter.</u>" However, Officer Bier's report does not say that Watkins stumbled and almost fell inside the store. In fact, the report indicates that the officer could only see Watkins from the shoulders up as he approached the counter. Impeachment by omission - meaning that the witness testified in court to something that was not in the report - it is a little harder to accomplish than a direct prior inconsistent statement, but it is still very doable.

Q: <u>You testified on direct</u> examination that you saw Mr. Watkins stumble and almost fall as he approached the counter inside from the store? (Credit prior statement's reliability)

A: Yes.

Q: You made a written report in this case within an hour of the incident, right?

A: Yes.

Q: I am handing the witness proposed exhibit #x.
         This is the report you made within a couple of hours after the incident, isn't it?

A: Yes.

Q: That is your signature on the report, isn't that true?

A: Yes

Q: <u>Even though you said on direct examination</u> that you saw Mr. Watkins <u>stumble and almost fall</u> as he approached the counter <u>inside</u> the store, <u>nowhere</u> in this report that you prepared <u>does</u> <u>it state</u> that you saw Watkins stumble and almost fall <u>inside</u> the store, does it? [If the witness takes time to look for it in the report, give them as much time as they want to take.

A: No, it doesn't say that.

The report says nothing about Watkins' behavior in the store. Behavior in the store is critical to proving that defendant Jones knew that Watkins was intoxicated.

Additional questions beyond the bare-bones foundation.
Lawyer could build up the report, for example:

> "You try to put everything that is important in the report, right?"
> "They taught you to do that in the department training, right?"

The potential re-direct examination:
If it were my witness who was impeached, my redirect would go something like this:

Q: Officer, how do you explain what seems to be an inconsistency between your direct testimony that Watkins stumbled inside the store and your report, which does not mention Watkins stumbled inside the store?

A: [Perhaps the best answer would be] I can't put everything into the report. But I clearly remember that he stumbled inside the store.

Impeachment by Inconsistent Oral Deposition

Assume the same factual inconsistency of testimony on direct examination that Mr. Watkins stumbled inside the store, but this time also assume that Officer Bier gave an oral deposition under oath and gave an answer that did not mention any stumbling inside the store.

After laying a foundation which would include the procedures involved in the deposition, such as:
- You came to my office?
- You took an oath to tell the truth?
- I told you that if you didn't understand the question, you should tell me you don't understand?
- You had an opportunity to review and correct the transcript some weeks after the deposition?
- After you read the typed deposition, you signed the deposition as being accurate?

then complete the impeachment by reading the questions that were asked and the answers that were given at the deposition.

The impeaching sequence could go something like this:

Q: Even though you said on direct that Watkins stumbled and almost fell in the store when he was at the counter, at your deposition weren't you asked this question, and didn't you give this answer:

Q: Now Officer Bier, how was Watkins walking when he was inside the store?
A: I can't say for sure. My view into the store was obstructed.

A: Yes, that is what it says.

You want to confine your questions to what the witness said at the deposition, not what the witness remembers now. Your opponent will no doubt do redirect examination to try to rehabilitate the witness.

Impeachment by Inconsistent Oral Deposition - Short Form

On direct examination, the witness said, "The light was green."
You want to impeach with the witness' deposition that says, "The light was red."

Q: On direct examination you said the light was green?
A: Yes.

Q: Even though on direct examination you said that the light was green, at the deposition weren't you asked the following question, and didn't you give the following answer?
      Q: What color was the light?
      A: The light was red.
A: Yes.

Impeachment by Inconsistent Oral Deposition - Long Form

On direct examination, the witness said, "The light was green."
You want to impeach with the witness' deposition that says,
"The light was red."

Highlight the Inconsistency
Q. On direct examination you said the light was green. [A: Yes]
Q.   There is no question in your mind about that? [A: No question.]

Lock the Witness into The Testimony (you can omit this step)
Q.   Have you ever said anything different? [No]
Q.   Are you sure it was green? [Yes]
Q.   Isn't it true that the light was in fact red? [No]

Build Up the Impeaching Document
Q. You remember coming to my office last year to answer some questions?
Q. You came for a deposition on July 11, last year?
Q. I asked you questions, and you gave me answers, isn't that right?
Q. Your lawyer sat next to you while you answered?
Q. A court reporter took down your answers?
Q. That reporter gave you an oath to tell the truth?
Q. You agreed to tell the truth?
Q. After that deposition, the Q's and A's were typed up and you had a chance to read it over?
Q. After making sure it was correct, you signed it didn't you?
Q. This is your signature, isn't it?
Q. This deposition was just four months after the accident?
Q. Even though on direct examination you said that the light was green, at the deposition weren't you asked the following question, and didn't you give the following answer?
    Q: What color was the light?
    A: The light was red.

Impeachment by Inconsistent Oral Statement

(Assuming only the cross-examining lawyer heard the inconsistent statement)

Assume that although Bier testified on direct exam that "Watkins stumbled and almost fell inside the store," Bier was overheard outside the courtroom say to a person who is not available to testify, "I never really saw Watkins stumble inside the store." However, only the lawyer for Cut-Rate Liquor heard Bier's statement.

This is an inconsistent oral statement. Unlike most inconsistent statements, this one was <u>not made prior</u> to the in-court testimony on direct exam. <u>This statement was made after</u> the in-court testimony.

This fact pattern presents a special problem if the lawyer was the only person who overhead the statement. If Bier denies making the statement, the cross-examiner does not have a witness who could be called to the stand to complete the impeachment of Bier. So, if no one other that the lawyer overhead the statement, what can the lawyer do? The lawyer certainly cannot testify in this case.

A suggestion would be to handle this problem by being as detailed as possible during the questioning leading up to the impeaching question. If the trier of fact believes the details, the trier of fact might believe that Bier also made the final statement ("I never saw him stumble inside the store.").

Detailed questioning

Q: During the break, you went outside the courtroom, didn't you?

Q: And you sat on the bench outside?

Q: You sat next to a man wearing a blue shirt, right?

Q: And the two of you had a conversation?

Q: You talked for about 5 minutes, right?

Q: "Even though you said on direct exam in court just 30 minutes ago that Watkins stumbled and almost fell in the store when he was at the counter, didn't you say to a man on a bench outside this courtroom just 10 minutes ago, "I never really saw Watkins stumble inside the store?"

Learned Treatises:
Use on Direct Exam to Support Your Expert
R803(18) – Hearsay Exception

After an expert testifies that it is not possible to determine if the plaintiff's epileptic seizures are caused by the plaintiff's auto accident, the following questioning takes place to use a learned treatise to support the expert's opinion. This is an example of using a "paper expert," or said another way, getting the opinion of two experts but only calling one as a witness.

Q: Dr. Rosenberg, are you familiar with the text called Medicine written by Dr. Mark Fishman?
A: Yes

Q: Let me show you proposed exhibit #1. What is it?
A: It is the book called Medicine written by Dr. Mark Fishman.

Q: Is it a recognized as a reliable authority in the field of medicine?
A: Yes

Q: What does the Fishman text say about the causes of epileptic seizures?
A: On page 135, Fishman says that a cause is found for seizures in less than 25% of the cases.

Using a learned treatise as a hearsay exception can <u>only done by reading</u> the treatise to the trier of fact, but <u>not by physically introducing</u> the treatise into evidence. R803(18)

(Discussion continued on the next page)

**RULE 803. Exceptions to the Rule Against Hearsay —
Regardless of Whether the Declarant Is Available as a Witness**
The following are not excluded by the rule against hearsay,
regardless of whether the declarant is available as a witness:
(18) Statements in Learned Treatises, Periodicals, or Pamphlets.
A statement contained in a treatise, periodical, or pamphlet if:

> **(A)** the statement is <u>called to the attention of an expert</u> witness
> on cross-examination or relied on by the expert on direct
> examination; and
> **(B)** the publication is established as a <u>reliable authority</u> by the
> expert's admission or testimony, by another expert's testimony,
> or by judicial notice.

If admitted, the statement may be <u>read</u> into evidence <u>but not
received</u> as an exhibit.

3 Key Points for Using the Learned Treatise

**To use a learned treatise on either direct or cross-examination,
under R803(18)**
1) there must be an expert <u>on the witness stand,</u>
2) the treatise has been established as a <u>reliable authority,</u> and
3) the statement may be <u>only read</u> into the record, but the treatise
cannot be physically introduced into evidence.

Learned Treatises:
Use on Cross to Attack
the Opposing Expert
R803(18) – Hearsay Exception

After establishing that Mark Fishman's text called "Medicine" is a reliable authority in the field of medicine, either by your expert, or by your opponent's expert, or by judicial notice (Note: judges seldom take judicial notice on this subject), the lawyer below uses the learned treatise on cross examination to contradict the opposing party's expert witness. A statement in a treatise can be used to impeach the opponent's expert and as substantive evidence (meaning for the truth of the statement – this is a hearsay exception).

Q: Dr. Barron, you testified during your direct examination that Mr. Fulbright's epilepsy was caused by the auto accident, right?
A: Yes.

Q: Dr., there is no medical evidence that Mr. Fulbright showed any clinical evidence of brain injury immediately after the incident is there?
A: That's correct.

Q: And no evidence of a skull fracture?
A: That's also correct.

Q: And no evidence of bloody spinal fluid, right?
A: Correct again.

Q: Dr., doesn't the text called, Medicine, written by Mark Fishman, indicate on page 132 that the four symptoms most commonly found with epileptic seizures are 1) loss of consciousness, 2) clinical evidence of brain injury immediately after the incident, 3) skull fracture, and 4) bloody spinal fluid?
A: Yeah, Fishman does say that.

Q: Your Honor, no further questions.

Voicemail, Phone Conversations, Recorded Phone Conversations

There is nothing special about the identification of a telephone call. Authentication for voice identification is covered in the R901(b)(5)&(6).

Do you know X?

How do you know X?

How long have you known X?

Have you ever spoken with X on the phone?

How often have you spoken with X on the phone?

On [the day in question] did you have a phone conversation with X?

Who initiated that call?

[If **your** witness initiated the call]

> How did you make the call? [Ans: used contacts list on cell phone; used recent call list on cell phone; used landline]

> Was their name already in your cell phone from previous calls to them?

> Did you recognize the voice when your call was answered?

> Who were you talking to?

(Continued on next page)

[If the **other party** initiated the call]

Could you tell who was calling you?

How could you tell who was calling you? [Name appeared on my cell phone]

Why did their name appear in your cell phone? [I had name in my contacts list from many previous calls]

Who was on the phone when you answered the call? [The defendant]

How did you know that? [We have talked many times before. I recognized his voice.]

What did he say during that call?

Digital Evidence
Electronically Stored Information – ESI

Electronically Stored Information (EIS) includes emails, text messages, websites, fax, social media, computer printouts, and other digital records. Although we evidence professors will tell you that the classic rules of evidence, created before cell phones, computers, and the Internet, are more than adequate for the new digital world, some people doubt it.

Yet truly, introducing digital evidence in court still does apply the same basic HARROWing principles found in all evidence codes – whether introducing physical item or digital evidence.

HARROWing my pneumonic to remind us of evidence principles to consider when introducing physical pieces of evidence, especially ones with words on or in them. HARROWing - defined as extremely distressing, agonizing, excruciating, torturing, painful, and causing physical or psychological pain – is how many new lawyers describe their experience trying to introduce evidence

H = Hearsay;
A= Authentication;
R= R401 relevancy (sometime called "logical relevancy);
R=R403 (sometimes called "legal Relevancy);
OW = Original Writings (traditionally known as Best Evidence).

The same rules of evidence apply to ESI as they do to paper and physical evidence. The most challenging foundational issues for digital evidence are establishing:1) who created the digital evidence (the author), and 2) has it been altered?

A Variety of Standards

Different standards have developed in various jurisdictions for authenticating digital evidence.

The Texas courts, and probably most jurisdictions, use an authentication standard identical to the standard used for traditional forms of evidence – "evidence sufficient to support a finding (R 901). The Texas standard can be thought of and remembered by the state's placement on a map – it is a lower standard.

However, the Maryland courts, and a few others, have developed a higher standard – like Maryland's placement on a map. Maryland courts seem to require that the proponent of digital evidence prove that the digital evidence has not been altered or hacked, it comes from a certain source, and that no one other than the owner could have used the electronic device to send or post the message. This view of EIS authentication is concerned about "voodoo information taken from the Internet." It creates a standard that can seldom be met.

The Grimm, Joseph & Capra article, Best Practices for Authenticating Digital Evidence 69 Baylor L.R. 1 (2017) is a great source for understanding factors in authenticating digital evidence. That article presents an overview of how Rules of Evidence 104(a) and 104(b) interact in the authentication process and argues that digital evidence should be authenticated requiring only evidence

<u>"sufficient to support a finding,"</u> - which is a low standard.

The authors offer the opinion that,

<u>"Generally speaking, it will be a rare case in which an item of digital evidence cannot be authenticated."</u>

The article covers various ways to authenticate digital evidence. Most helpful will be the examples of various types of circumstantial evidence that would qualify as "distinctive characteristics" under R901(b)(4). Additional, less frequently used methods of authenticating evidence are also covered, such as, personal knowledge of a witness, business records (in some email situations), jury comparison, and production in discovery.

Distinctive Characteristics and Circumstantial Evidence Used to Authenticate Emails and Text Messages as having been sent by a particular person or as having been received by a particular person

There are many possible ways to use circumstantial evidence to qualify as "distinctive characteristics" to authenticate Electronically Stored Information (ESI) under R901(b)(4) Distinctive Characteristics and the Like. Appearance, contents, substance, internal patterns, or other distinctive characteristics of the item taken together with all the circumstances are almost endless.

The Grimm, Joseph & Capra article offers many extremely valuable suggestions about circumstantial evidence which can be considered "distinctive characteristics" and used to authenticate digital evidence under R901(b)(4).

For example, when laying the foundation for an email or text, consider:
1) information in or about the email or text
2) information outside the email or text itself that leads back to the author
3) forensic information, and
4) information outside the email or text itself indicating receipt of the message.

Factors suggested by Grimm, Joseph, and Capra used to authenticate authorship or receipt of a message include:

1) information in or about the email or text, such as:
- the email address, email signature, a nickname, a screen name, initials, a moniker, the author's customary use of emoji or emoticons, a writing style (including phrases and abbreviations frequently used by the author), referring to facts only the author or small group of people would know about, facts uniquely tied to the author, information about the author's family, photos of the author, items of importance to the author such as a car or a pet, and other such information

2) information outside the email or text itself that leads back to the author, such as:

- the email was part of a chain or series of emails from the same person, the claimed author told the witness to expect an email from the author, the author orally repeats its content soon after the email is sent, the author discusses the contents of the email with the third party, the author leaves a voicemail substantially of the same content, and other such information

3) forensic information, such as:

- an email's hash values or testimony from a forensic witness that the email came from a particular device at a particular time, and other such information

4) information outside the email or text itself indicating receipt of the message, such as:

- a reply was received by the sender that came from the recipient, later conduct of the recipient reflects knowledge of the contents of the sent message, later communication of the recipient reflects knowledge of the message, and the message was received and accessed on an electronic device in the possession of the recipient, and other such information.

Presenting the Digital Evidence
from a Cell Phone in Court

- Print the page from the phone and use the printout in court.
- If a photo comes from a cell phone, attach the picture to an email, and then print from a computer.
- Screenshot the information (picture, text message, email, social media post), email it, then print from a computer.

Self-Authentication for Digital Evidence

Recent amendments to the Federal Rules of Evidence allow for self-authentication of certified records
  – See FRE 902(13)&(14)

Digital Evidence and Self-Authentication

R902(11) Self-authentication
Certified Domestic Records of a Regularly Conducted Activity.
The original or a copy of a domestic record that meets the requirements of Rule 803(6)(A)-(C), as shown by a certification of the custodian or another qualified person that complies with a federal statute or a rule prescribed by the Supreme Court. Before the trial or hearing, the proponent must give an adverse party reasonable written notice of the intent to offer the record — and must make the record and certification available for inspection — so that the party has a fair opportunity to challenge them.

> Many states have created forms for self-authentication of business records or have court rules which cover certifications for business records.

FRE 902(13) (Added to FRE Dec. 2017)
(13) Certified Records Generated by an Electronic Process or System. A record generated by an electronic process or system that produces an accurate result, as shown by a certification of a qualified person that complies with the certification requirements of Rule 902(11) or (12). The proponent must also meet the notice requirements of Rule 902(11).
>   [JB: covers text messages, cell phone photos,
>   GPS data, and other ESI]

FRE 902(14) Certified Data Copied from an Electronic Device, Storage Medium, or File. Data copied from an electronic device, storage medium, or file, if authenticated by a process of digital identification, as shown by a certification of a qualified person that complies with the certification requirements of Rule 902(11) or (12). The proponent also must meet the notice requirements of Rule 902(11).

Email – Witness is the Sender (Outgoing Email)

Q: How did you notify Cut-Rate about …

A: I sent an email to Dan Jones

Q: What email address did you use?

A: DJones@Cutrate.com

Q: How do you know that was the correct address?

A: He and I have email back and forth for a few months, and all of his emails to me came from that email address

Q: Let me show you what has been marked as plaintiff's proposed exhibit #1.

Q: What is it? (A printout of the email I sent to Jones that day.).

Q: How do you know that? (I wrote it. I remember it. It was in my "sent mail" folder.)

Q: Your Honor I offer the exhibit into evidence.

Email – Witness is the Recipient (Incoming Email)

Do you know Dan Jones?

How do you know him?

Are you familiar with the email address DJones@Cutrate.com?

Have you received emails from Dan Jones in the past?

Have you sent emails to Dan Jones at that address?

Has he responded to your emails from that email address?

Is that email address in your email contacts?

In late April, did you receive an email from Dan Jones about selling liquor?

Did you recognize email address as being from Dan Jones?

I am handing you what has been marked as proposed exhibit #7. You recognize it?

What is it? (A: The email from Dan Jones)

Why would you say that's an email from Dan Jones? [provides information about distinctive characteristics of this email]

How did you get a paper copy of this email? (A: I printed it out.)

Is this a true and accurate printout of that email?

Your Honor, I offer the proposed exhibit into evidence.

> [The email reads: "I might be getting fired. They caught me selling booze to drunks again."]

Text Message

Received by Witness

Do you know Y?

Do you communicate with Y on a regular basis?

In what ways to you communicate with Y?

Did you receive a text message from the Y [recently; on or about _ date, on the topic of ..., etc.]?

Would you recognize a printout of the message if you were to see it again?

Let me show you what has been marked as proposed exhibit # 1. Do you recognize it?

What is it? [Ans: A screenshot from my cell phone]

How do you know that this is a message from Y? [It is similar to other messages I have received from Y in that ...]

How did it appear when it arrived on your phone? [Showed up under the name and with the picture I had previously assigned to Y]

What other distinctive characteristics did you notice about the message? [provide as many as distinctive characteristics possible]

Is it a fair and accurate representation of the text message you received [recently; on or about _ date, on the topic of visiting your son, etc.]?

Has it been altered in any way?

I would like to enter the proposed exhibit into evidence

Social Media
Facebook, Instagram, Snapchat, Twitter, and other Posts

Do you know B?

How long have you known him?

Are you familiar with Facebook?

Does B have a Facebook account?

Have you seen posts by B on his Facebook account in the past?

How do you know that B made those posts? [provide distinctive characteristics]

Have you seen a posting on B's Facebook account about [the matter in question]?

Let the record reflect that I am handing you what has been marked as proposed exhibit 12 and ask if you can identify it?

What is it?

Is that a screenshot of the Facebook posting by B about ___?

What day did you take the screenshot?

Is it a true and accurate screenshot of that posting?

Is the post still on B's account? [Ask this question only if it is currently on the account.]

I offer the proposed exhibit into evidence.

Internet Website – Web Posting

Did you visit Professor John Barkai's webpage? [Yes]

How did you access it? [Googled "John Barkai" on my phone]

How did you find his page?
    Ans: I clicked on the link that said "Prof. John Barkai Homepage."

What did you find when you clicked on that link for the homepage?
    Ans: I found his list of courses and other posts.

Did you click on any particular link?
    Ans: I clicked Hawaii Rules of Evidence (HRE) Book Page

What did you find on that page when you clicked on it?
        A: I found a link to buy from Amazon a copy of this Rules of Evidence Handbook.

Let me show you what's been marked as proposed exhibit # 14. Can you identify it?
        A: Yes. It's a screenshot of that webpage with instructions about how to buy a copy of this book from Amazon.

Was that screenshot a print of the page from his website?
        A: Yes, I printed it myself.

Is this exhibit a fair and accurate copy of that webpage?   [Yes]

Has this exhibit of the screenshot been altered or otherwise change from the image on your phone in any way?   [No]

I offer the exhibit into evidence.

Fax – Incoming

Does your office have a fax machine?

Do you send outgoing faxes?

Do you receive incoming faxes?

Have you received purchase orders from the defendant by fax in the past?

Let me show you plaintiff's proposed exhibit # 27 and ask if you can identify it? [A: Yes. I can]

What is it? [A: A fax I received about six months ago from the defendant]

Why do you say this fax came from the defendant?
A: There are number of factors in addition to the document being written on the defendant's letterhead stationery. The fax is signed by the head of defendant's purchasing department, and I am familiar with her signature from our past dealings. Further, imprinted on the bottom of this fax sheet is the fax number for the defendant's company, and I have faxed prior documents to the defendant by using that number. Finally, the document relates to the purchase of some equipment that I had discussed with the defendant's head of purchasing just a few hours before the fax arrived at my office.

Is this document in the same or substantially the same condition as it was when you received it?   [A: Yes, it is exactly the same.]

There have been no alterations or changes? [A: None whatsoever.]

Your Honor, I move that this proposed exhibit be admitted into evidence.

Expert Opinions

Four Part Expert Opinion Foundation and Testimony

1. Background and qualifications
2. Tender / Offer as expert
   – Opponent's voir dire (testing qualifications)
3. Opinion / Conclusion (standard?) R702
4. Basis for opinion R703
   – Including reasonable reliance on inadmissible evidence
   – disclosure of inadmissible evidence?

Three Simple Questions

1) Q: "Do you have an opinion as to whether...

2) Q: "What is that opinion?"

3) Q: "How did you reach that opinion?
   A: [including inadmissible information reasonably relied upon by experts in the particular field, R703]

How to Start

The expert witness examination normally starts with questions to establish the witness' qualifications to testify as an expert.

Topics for Background and Qualifications of an Expert:

- formal education, work experience, number of previous times retained, qualified, and testified as an expert, in which courts, on-the-job training, non-degree training courses, publications in the field, teaching in the field, memberships in related professional associations, and any other topics relevant to showing the person is an expert.

Tender / Offer

After presenting the expert's background and qualifications, in jurisdictions where the judge must "certify" or "find" that the witness is an expert and is to permitted to testify as an expert, the lawyer presenting the expert then "tenders" or "offers" the witness to the judge as an expert, stating the field of expertise.

"I offer/tender Mr. X as an expert in the field of…"

"I ask the court to certify Ms. Y as an expert in the field of …"

Can you call the expert an "expert?"

After any voir dire (a limited cross examination to test the qualifications of the witness) by opposing counsel and objections, the judge rules on whether the expert can continue to testify as an expert. Some courts do not allow the lawyer to use the word "expert" to refer to the expert witness. but the judge is still changed with the responsibility of determining if the witness is qualified as an expert. Yet no one uses the word "expert" in front of lay fact finders. The apparent reason for such a practice is, as explained below.

The 2000 Advisory Committee Notes to the amendment to Federal Rule of Evidence 702 says, in part:

"…The use of the term "expert" in the Rule does not, however, mean that a jury should actually be informed that a qualified witness is testifying as an "expert." Indeed, there is much to be said for a practice that prohibits the use of the term "expert" by both the parties and the court at trial. Such a practice "ensures that trial courts do not inadvertently put their stamp of authority" on a witness's opinion, and protects against the jury's being "overwhelmed by the so-called 'experts'."

More Tenders/Offers of the expert

"We believe that Mr. Taylor should be permitted to offer his opinions in this case."

"I tender Dr. Barron as an expert in the field of family medicine and request that she be allowed to testify as such.

"I offer Dr. Rosenberg as an expert in the field of neurology."

"Judge, we ask that the court accept Dr. Shigeta as an expert in civil engineering."

Offering the Opinion

Traditionally, the opinion is delivered in a two questions sequence:

Q1: Do you have an opinion as ....?

A: Yes

Q2: What is that opinion?

"Do you have an opinion, <u>within a reasonable degree of scientific certainty,</u> as to the time of death of Ms. X?"

"Do you have an opinion, <u>to a reasonable degree of medical probability,</u> as to whether the motorcycle accident caused Mr. Fulbright's epilepsy?"

"Do you have an opinion, <u>to a reasonable degree of engineering certainty,</u> as to whether the XXX caused the bridge to fail?"

"Do you have an opinion whether Mr. X suffered a brain damage as a result of the fight?"

Standards for Stating an Expert's Opinion

There are no minimum standards under R702 describing how "good" an expert's opinion must be to be stated in court. By case law, some courts and jurisdictions require that the standard must be stated to a

"reasonable degree of [medical] <u>certainty,</u>" or a

"reasonable degree of [scientific] <u>probability.</u>"

Other jurisdictions simply allow an expert to state an opinion without any specific qualification.

"What did your examination reveal?"

The above standards of "certainty" and "probability" are vague and rather unhelpful standards to a lay jury or courts-martial member who might be able to understand percentages, but who is given no guidance to the certainty or probability. Do those standards mean 51%, 65%, 75%, 85%, 95%, etc.? "Preponderance of the evidence" does have an associated percentage (50%+), but terms such as "sufficient to support a finding," "clear and convincing," "beyond a reasonable doubt," as well as "certainty" and "probability" do not. Simply, use whatever standard your judge and jurisdiction require.

In an attempt to be persuasive, some lawyers ask the experts questions like:

"How positive are you of your opinion?"
"What is the degree of your certainty?"

Inadmissible Information Reasonably Relied Upon

Experts can base their opinions on hearsay and other inadmissible evidence. R703 says in part:

"If experts in the particular field would reasonably rely on those kinds of facts or data in forming an opinion on the subject, they need not be admissible for the opinion to be admitted."

You should have in your tool chest of questions this question.
"Is that the type of information reasonably relied upon by experts in your field?

Remember

Whoever has the Biggest, Most Qualified Expert Might Win

Because opposing parties often have opposing experts, who have reached opposing conclusions, the advocacy principle is for you to try to present a more qualified and more credible expert than your opponent's expert. If "your" expert's testimony and conclusions are believed on the issue that the experts are testifying about, you are more likely to win your case.

Humor in Trial Evidence:
Cartoon Caption Contest Winners

Since the fall of 1980, I have been putting cartoons on my law school final exams and asking students to write original captions for those cartoons related to the topic of our class – that is about 25 years before the New Yorker Magazine started running its cartoon captioning contest. I have used these captioning contests in my evidence, litigation, and negotiation and ADR classes.

By the end of summer 2020, I hope to have the two cartoon captioning books available on Amazon for purchase at cost.

Humor in Trial Evidence:
Cartoon Caption Contest Winners and Challenges
from My Evidence Class

Humor in Negotiations & ADR:
Cartoon Caption Contest Winners from the
ABA Dispute Resolution Magazine

The above books are among the most creative work I have done in the academic world. I sell them at cost to get them wide distribution and to allow other teachers, trainers, and presenters to add a little humor to their presentations. Others might be just entertained by these publications.

For 40 years I have used these captioning contests on my final exams with the instructions: "Please write one or more captions for these cartoons. All captions written in English receive full credit." Within the two books, I have reproduced about 1,000 of the funniest (to me) captions. I use the captioned cartoons in my future classes and presentations, and they are a nice little gift I send to any guest speakers who appeared in my class the previous semester. I hope you enjoy the following sample of captioned cartoons.

I can grant you permission to use any of the captions; the cartoons belong to the artists and the organizations that own the rights to the cartoons. I got permission from them for my use. However, if you are using them for class or other educational purposes, you can probably claim "fair use."

Artist Misha Richter

"What a coincidence, my lawyer had Barkai for evidence too!"

"You know Larry, I don't think I'd make the best character witness for you."

"My lawyer was wrong! That stuff was admissible the whole time."

P1: "We should hang sometime."
P2: "Yeah. What your cell number?"

"So, it turns out the right to confront witnesses against you doesn't include threatening them with a gun."

"Well if we've learned anything, I guess we shouldn't have updated our escape route on twitter and Facebook."

Artist Joseph Mirachi

"Crawford...Smawford. Let's just admit it!" (confrontation)

"He must be one of Barkai's evidence students."

"Shall we take judicial notice that this lawyer has no idea what he is talking about?" R201

"Thanks to rule 403, we've still got time for a round of golf this afternoon."

"Do you remember how we decided whether the statement was testimonial or not testimonial last time? Was it darts or a coin toss?" (confrontation)

Artist Rex May

"So apparently these days the spousal testimonial privilege belongs only to the testifying spouse." R505

"We should have studied more for the evidence exam!"

"I thought grand jury testimony was admissible under a hearsay exception. Crawford changed that?"

"This isn't what I thought the judge meant when she talked about the "chain of custody." R901

"With all those evidence rules, you'd think they'd get us out of here with one of them!"

Artist Tim O'Brien

"I don't think Sally is going to go for a hearsay catchall exception." R807

"I wish there was a rule allowing us to smack their heads every time they make those long objections."

"What exactly is collateral again?" (impeachment)

"Do you think they should have given a limiting instruction below? Why bother, the jurors aren't going to understand them anyway." R106

Artist Mallory Hee (my research assistant)

"Can we take judicial notice that the bar results are out, and new lawyers will soon appear before us making bad objections?" R201, R103

"Who are we to judge?"

"They "restyled" the rules of evidence. Don't you think it's time they restyled the robes?"

"Do you remember the difference between adjudicative facts and legislative facts?" R201

J1: "He has a habit of getting on my nerves."
J2: "No, that's just his character." R404, R406

"Psst ... I still don't understand hearsay." R801

Artist Mike Twony

"Well, Your Honor, I think it's pretty clear that I'm an expert in all things "Viking." R702

"Absolutely! The defendant has a reputation in our community for peacefulness. Unlike most of us, he sometimes refrains from pillaging the women and children when we go on our daily raids of nearby villages." R404 R608

"Are you competent to speak for Viking traditions?" R601 R702

"Your Honor, I can't say it's my modus operandi alone. For centuries, thousands of other Vikings have raided, pillaged, and conquered villages." R404(b)

Photoshopped by John Barkai

"Why didn't Scalia just tell us what testimonial is?" (confrontation)

"Heads says, "The probative value outweighs its prejudicial effect," tails says, "It doesn't." R403

"I think people are starting to catch on that even we don't really know how presumptions work." R301

For the life of me, I have no idea what is admissible. I just fake it."

"Where does Snapchat fit into the best evidence rule?"

Artist Mark Anderson

"I'm afraid the Confrontation Clause only guarantees the right to cross examine live witnesses."

"If we ignore your prior convictions that are more than 10 years old, I suppose we can let you in." R609(b)

"It says here, as a lawyer, you once argued that the Bible lacks "sufficient guarantees of trustworthiness." R807

"Well, I do remember all my hearsay exceptions." R803 R804

Photoshopped by John Barkai

"Wannabe Experts Beware the Daubert Gatekeeper. R702

"Come any closer and I'll see that you are unavailable to testify." R804

"Oh, I'll tell you about confrontation!" (Crawford)

"A brick may not be a wall, but it's still impressive - like me." R401

Photoshopped by John Barkai (my dogs)

"Authenticate yourself." R901

Q: "What happened to you?"
A: "I broke my chain of custody." R901

Daubert meets Frye. R702

"And then he told me, "I'd settle for a bone." R408, R801(d)(2)

"I planned to be unavailable, but my owner named me "Say" so I got confused when I thought he called me from the courthouse steps – Here Say."

Photoshopped by John Barkai

"Got it. Make him "unavailable." R804

"Are you trying to impeach me by prior bad acts? Say your dying declaration." R404 R608 R609 R803

"Are you sure you want to confront me?" (Crawford)

"I love steroids and the FRE."

Artist Mallory Hee

"Just don't make a habit out of it." R406

"You know, privilege doesn't matter if I choose to testify against you for pooping on the carpet." PR505

I'm offended the judge thinks fetching the paper every day is "unreflective behavior." R406

"She told me she was a purebred."

"Yes, the fact that you always pee on every fire hydrant on Main Street every time you go out in the morning can be used against you! No, no one has to see you do it. It's what they call habit." R406

Artist Mallory Hee; photoshopped by John Barkai

"To hell with relevancy! Ask him what he ate at McDonalds!" R401

"But, your honor! Bias is never COW-lateral. It is always MOO-terial." (bias)

"Is it true you work for the USDA?"

"How could any of you believe that he's a better expert on the digestive system than me? He only has one stomach." R702

"Now that is an excited udderance!" R803(3)

Artist Mallory Hee

"And finally, your Honor, I object to you!"

"I'd like to retract my admission, please". R801(d)(2)

"Did you hear the one about Officer Bier and the bottle of Thunderbird wine?"

Good lawyers get evidence thrown out under Rule 403; great lawyers get opposing counsel thrown out. R403

Who is Crawford, and why can't I testify about his "testimonial statements?"

Artist Mallory Hee

"Sure, I know of the cat's reputation. He's a bad cat." R404

"Yeah, he does have a reputation for truthfulness. He lies like a dog." R608

"Those aren't distinctive characteristics. All dogs have fleas." R901(b)

"I don't believe in dog, but I will tell the truth." (Dyslexic witness taking the oath.) "R603 R610

Photoshopped by John Barkai

"Well, I received my Doctor of Veterinary Sciences degree from the Rin Tin Tin School of Veterinary Sciences and did a residency at the Lassie Clinic Massachusetts. Since then I been sniffing around and writing health articles for Milk-Bone." (Qualifying an expert witness) R 702

"Of course it's biased testimony. He's man's best friend."

"The rules say you can't impeach him, but everyone knows he'll lie like a dog."

"Objection. Here boy! Oh, I mean hearsay." R801

Artist Mallory Hee

"Daubert has turned this place into a zoo." R702

"Ask him leading questions. He's used to being on a leash. R611

"He's biased. On cross, ask him if he ever ate my homework."

"Sure, he is my best friend, but couldn't you have thought up a better character witness for me?" R404

Artist Mike Shapiro; photoshopped by John Barkai

"Your bedtime story tonight is the Federal Rules of Evidence. That should put you to sleep quickly."

"Dad, Timmy said Santa doesn't exist." "Girls, that's just hearsay." R801

Girls, was the picture you drew of me at school today a fair and accurate representation? R901

"Girls, I'd like to tell you all about my day, but everyone Daddy talks to at work is part of a privileged relationship." R501

Artist Mallory Hee

"Of course it was a dying declaration. I ate him, didn't I?" R804(2)

"I can't help it if everything people say when I am around is an excited utterance. R803(2)

"Because you didn't ask permission to approach me, I'm going to snap."

"It was self-defense. The lady in the boat said she would just kill for an alligator bag."

Artist Mark Anderson

"Well sir, it looks like that drunken marriage in Vegas was good for something. Everything you said to her that week before the divorce will remain confidential at trial." R501

"Of course, even you would be considered a competent witness." R601

"Shh! Don't say a word. There is no attorney-client privilege here. The office is bugged and we're in a strict common law jurisdiction." R501

"Dave, I asked for a memo on why he's guilty. You can't just hand me paper that says, "Because he is."

Photoshopped by John Barkai

"O.K. Heads we'll call it "hearsay" and tails is "not hearsay."
R801

"So, I asked my son about the dent in the car and he replied,
"Subsequent remedial measures are irrelevant." R407

"You tell me. I got a C+ in Evidence."

"I wish I had paid more attention in Evidence class."

Artist Mark Anderson

"No counsel Snapchats do not qualify as photographic evidence since it lives in the cloud and disappears." R901

"Counselor, I highly doubt that "Bone Fractures for Dummies" is a reliable authority in the field of medicine." R803(18)

"So, Your Honor, you are saying we opened up the door when I was talking about how truthful Mr. Grimes was? Well, I would request that Your Honor closes the door at this time."

Artist Mark Anderson

"The first thing my father told me was hearsay."

I'm here, but I have no memory. Am I "unavailable" as a witness?"   R804

"And then the professor said there were over 20 exceptions to the hearsay rule. It was horrifying!" R 801, 803, 804

"Yes, I am a lawyer, and I do want to know exactly how confidential is this session? Are there any exceptions?"

Photoshopped by John Barkai and Cartoonized

You aren't an expert unless I say so." R702

"The best evidence in your case would be for you to keep your mouth shut." R1001

"I don't care how many objections Professor Barkai taught you, none of them apply here!"

"If you don't stop asking leading questions on direct exam, the bailiff will be leading you into a jail cell." R611

Artist Chon Day

**"I think I'll be getting out soon.
My new lawyer had Professor Barkai for evidence."**

Humor in Negotiations & ADR:
Cartoon Caption Contest Winners from the
ABA Dispute Resolution Magazine

For 14 years (1997-2011), I ran the cartoon captioning contest, called "The Lighter Side," for the ABA's ADR Section Dispute Resolution Magazine (DRM). I have almost 500 "winning" captions for 54 cartoons that were published in the Magazine. Those cartoons and captions are essence of the book, Humor in Negotiations & ADR: Cartoon Caption Contest Winners from the ABA Dispute Resolution Magazine which is available on Amazon at cost. The captions published by the ABA are supplemented with "winning" captions from my final exams in negotiation & ADR classes.

The cartoon books are among the most creative work I have done in the academic world. I sell them at cost to get them wide distribution and to allow other teachers, trainers, and presenters to add a little humor to their presentations. Others might be just entertained by these publications.

For 40 years I have used these captioning contests on my final exams with the instructions: "Please write one or more captions for these cartoons. All captions written in English receive full credit." Within the cartoon books, I have reproduced about 1,000 of the funniest (to me) captions. I use the captioned cartoons in my future classes and presentations, and they are a nice gift for guest speakers in my class. I hope you enjoy them.

I can grant you permission to use any of the captions; the cartoons belong to the artists and the organizations that own the rights to the cartoons. I got permission to use them. However, if you are using them for class, training, or other educational purposes, you can probably claim "fair use." Consult a lawyer. You probably know some.

Artist W.B. Park

Is that offer to mediate still open?

"This isn't what I quite envisioned by the ADR challenge."

"My attorney says I shouldn't back down. What does yours say?"

"Our mediator is late. Should we start without him?

"Ah, now I get why you wanted to mediate."

"I'm kind of feeling under the weather today. Can we do ADR instead?

Artist Jeff Dionise

"It may be too late for active listening."

"Let's try good cop bad cop. You go out roaring and snarling, and I'll be along in a while."

"But I don't like your proposal of me going out to meet him halfway"

"Do you think he would agree to have Yogi mediate?"

"You said be stubborn. You said don't split the difference. If we had handed over Bambi, we wouldn't be in this mess."

"What's that transformational thing everyone's been talking about?"

"Now do you understand the mediator's point about WATNA?"

"He says, "Come out!" because he just wants to talk, but I don't believe him."

"I asked for a 'mediator,' but they sent a 'meat eater."

Artist Dan Mazanec

"Can we change to interest based negotiations? I don't like my position."

"Would you mind telling me where you received your ADR training?"

"We have ways of making you tell us your bottom line."

Thanks to new technology, Getting to Yes just got easier and faster.

Mediator Methods: Facilitate, Evaluate, and Intimidate - "Now do you want to settle?"

"Now, exactly what is your BATNA?"

Artist Jeff Dionise

"As a mediator, you're supposed to improve the lines of communication, not weigh them down."

"OK, this is a process known as "Online" mediation."

"Bottom line just won't bend, huh?"

"You want to "expand the pie?" It looks like you ate the pie.

"How can we negotiate a deal when you won't budge from your bottom line?"

"I can't believe that it was only a year ago that she took that negotiation class! Now, she is getting all the worms!"

Communication to prevent conflict: "No honey, I don't think you are gaining weight.

FRE Cross Reference Guide

Primary Rule	Refers to Rule:	Primary rule referred to by:
101	1101	502
104		1008 1101
403		609
404	412 607 608 609	
412		404
413	415	
414	415	414
415	413 414	413 414
501		502
502	101 501 1101	
602	703	
607		404
608	609	404
609	403	404 608
613	801(d)(2)	
701	702	
702		701
703		602
801	613 806	
803(10)	902	
803(24)	807	807 902
804(a)	804(b)(1)&(6) 804(b)(2)&(3)&(4)	
804(b)	807	807
806	801(d)(2)(C)	
807	803 804	
902		803 1105
1004		1008
1005	902(4)	1008
1008	104(b) 1004 1005	
1101	104(a)	101 502

Other Evidence Handbooks in this Series
by John Barkai

Evidentiary Foundations (2019)

Arizona Rules of Evidence Handbook with Common Objections & Evidentiary Foundations (2020)

California Rules of Evidence Handbook with Common Objections & Evidentiary Foundations (2020)

Chuuk Rules of Evidence Handbook with Common Objections & Evidentiary Foundations (2019)

Federal Rules of Evidence Handbook with Common Objections & Evidentiary Foundations (2020)

Federated States of Micronesia Rules of Evidence Handbook with Common Objections & Evidentiary Foundations (2019)

Florida Evidence Code Handbook with Common Objections & Evidentiary Foundations (2020)

Hawaii Rules of Evidence Handbook (2018)

Hawaii Rules of Evidence Handbook with Common Objections & Evidentiary Foundations (2020)

Humor in Negotiations & ADR: Cartoon Caption Contest Winners from the ABA Dispute Resolution Magazine (2020)

Humor in Trial Evidence: Cartoon Caption Contest Winners and Challenges from My Evidence Class (2020)

Illinois Rules of Evidence Handbook with Common Objections & Evidentiary Foundations (2020)

Kosrae Rules of Evidence Handbook with Common Objections & Evidentiary Foundations (2019)

Marshall Islands Rules of Evidence Handbook with Common Objections & Evidentiary Foundations (2019)

Michigan Rules of Evidence Handbook with Common Objections & Evidentiary Foundations (2020)

Military Rules of Evidence Handbook with Common Objections & Evidentiary Foundations (2020)

New Jersey Rules of Evidence Handbook with Common Objections & Evidentiary Foundations (2020)

Ohio Rules of Evidence Handbook with Common Objections & Evidentiary Foundations (2020)

Pennsylvania Rules of Evidence Handbook with Common Objections & Evidentiary Foundations (2020)

(Pennsylvania) Just the Rules: Pennsylvania of Evidence (2020)

The Pocket Guide to Common Trial Objections & Evidentiary Foundations (2020)

Pohnpei Rules of Evidence Handbook with Common Objections & Evidentiary Foundations (2019)

Texas Rules of Evidence Handbook with Common Objections & Evidentiary Foundations (2020)

(Texas) Just the Rules: Texas of Evidence (2020)

Virginia Rules of Evidence Handbook with Common Objections & Evidentiary Foundations (2020)

Yap Rules of Evidence Handbook with Common Objections & Evidentiary Foundations (2019)

All the above books are (or will be shortly) available exclusively on Amazon.com and are "print-on-demand."

To find Barkai's evidence handbooks,

1. Go to the Amazon website – www.Amazon.com
2. Change the tab on the left side of the search bar from "All" to "Books,"
3. Enter - Barkai evidence

History and Restyling of the Federal Rules of Evidence

The Federal Rules of Evidence (FRE) were adopted in 1975. Approximately 46 states have adopted evidence codes, by statute or court rule, which are patterned on the FRE. The states without FRE based evidence codes are California, Kansas, Missouri, and New York. The California Evidence Code took effect in 1965 and is quite different in structure than any other state evidence code.

Although most states modeled their evidence rules after the FRE, almost every state has some evidence provisions which are different from the federal rules and some states have very significant differences.

The FRE were "restyled" in 2011 to
> "make them more easily understood and to make style and terminology consistent throughout the rules. These changes are intended to be stylistic only. There is no intent to change any result in any ruling on evidence admissibility.... The [Restyling] Committee made special efforts to reject any purposed style improvement that might result in a substantive change in the application of a rule." --- See Restyled Rules Committee Note for Restyled Rules of Evidence.

So far, at least thirteen (13) states, have restyled their rules of evidence: Arizona (2012), Delaware (2017), Idaho (2018), Indiana (2013), Iowa (2017), Maine (2015), Mississippi (2016), New Hampshire (2017), Pennsylvania (2013), South Dakota (2016), Texas (2014), Utah (2012), and West Virginia (2014). The Military (2013) and the Commonwealth of the Northern Mariana Islands (2015) have also restyled.

An excellent resource for understanding the differences between the FRE and the evidence rules of other states is the multi-volume treatise, Wharton's Criminal Evidence by Bergman and Hollander. This treatise is available in many law libraries and is available on Westlaw, where it is called CRIMEVID database. Despite included the word "Criminal" in its title, the treatise discusses evidence issues (criminal and civil) but does not cover FRE 407, 408, and 411, and it does not cover the criminal topic of confrontation.

State Rules of Evidence Chart

	State	Unique Rules X=no	If FRE-Like Restyled in
1	Alabama	X	
2	Alaska	X	
3	Arizona	X	2012
4	Arkansas	X	
5	California	CEC 1-1605	
6	Colorado	X	
7	Connecticut	X	
8	Delaware	X	2017
9	Florida	FS: 92.05 to 70	
10	Georgia	U 24-1-1 to 14-3	
11	Hawaii	X	
12	Idaho	X	2018
13	Illinois	X	
14	Indiana	X	2013
15	Iowa	Iowa Court Rules: 5.101 to 5.1103	2017
16	Kansas	KS: 60-401 to 485	
17	Kentucky	X	
18	Louisiana	X	
19	Maine	X	2015
20	Maryland	X	
21	Massachusetts	X	
22	Michigan	X	
23	Minnesota	X	
24	Mississippi	X	2016
25	Missouri	§ 490.010 to .733	
26	Montana	X	
27	Nebraska	X	
28	Nevada	NV ST Ch 47-56	
29	New Hampshire	X	2017
30	New Jersey	X	

31	New Mexico	X	
32	New York*	No formal rules but a New York Guide to Evidence is maintained on the internet by the New York Courts	
33	North Carolina	X	
34	North Dakota	X	
35	Ohio	X	
36	Oklahoma	X	
37	Oregon	X 40.010 to .585	
38	Pennsylvania	X	2013
39	Rhode Island	X	
40	South Carolina	X	
41	South Dakota	X	2016
42	Tennessee	X	
43	Texas	X	2014
44	Utah	x	2012
45	Vermont	X	
46	Virginia	X	
47	Washington	X	
48	West Virginia	X	2014
40	Wisconsin	X	
50	Wyoming	X	

*New York is unusual in that it has no formal rules of evidence but the New York State Unified Court System has produced a set of rules that looks similar to the Federal Rules of Evidence but is only a "Guide." That N.Y. Guide is copyrighted by the courts and is not published in hard copy, and is found only the internet. No one is authorized to publish a hard copy of the internet.

Federal and State Caseload Statistics

Federal court cases are only a very small percentage, approximately 1%, of the total number of cases in American courts.

The most recent summary by the National Center for State Courts reports the filling of 84 million state court cases (including the 50 states, the District of Columbia, Puerto Rico, and Guam). That caseload statistic includes 45 million traffic cases, almost 18 million criminal cases, 15 million civil cases, 5 million domestic relations cases, and over 1 million juvenile cases. The number of state court cases has fallen to that level from a high of almost 104 million cases in 2007.

Federal courts report the filing of approximately 400,000 criminal and civil cases per year, not including almost 700,000 bankruptcy cases filed in the 12 months ending in June 2020 – which is very likely to increase with the pandemic. Of course not many of the bankruptcy cases have trials. Additionally, bankruptcy filings are down from approximately 1.5 million cases filed in 2008.

Why Did You Buy This Book?

I don't know why you bought this book. While it is possible that you are a lawyer who anticipates trying a case in federal court, that is unlikely because the vast majority of court cases are state cases, not federal cases. My guess is that you are a law school or researcher who is studying the Federal Rules of Evidence. The objections and evidentiary foundations sections make this handbook a great resource for clinics, trial practice courses, and mock trial competitors.

Dedication

To my wife Linda ,and my adult twin daughters Hope, and Leah,

who bring me so much joy

and enrich my life

and

to the hundreds of my former evidence and clinical students

who learned these rules of evidence with me

over the past 40 plus years

at the William S. Richardson School of Law

at the University of Hawaii.

About the Author

Teaching Evidence Since 4 B.C.

John Barkai has been teaching evidence since 4 B.C. – that is 4
years "Before Computers" were used at the University of Hawaii
Law School. He is a former Detroit Michigan criminal trial lawyer, a
fulltime law professor for over 45 years, and a Professor of Law at
the William S. Richardson School of Law at the University of
Hawaii for more than 40 years. He has taught evidence since 1981
and has been the Director, and now Co-Director, of the Law
School's Clinical Program since 1978. He has been a member of the
Hawaii Supreme Court's Standing Committee on the Rules of
Evidence since 1993. He has a B.B.A, M.B.A, and J.D, all from the
University of Michigan. For the past 47 years, he has taught a
criminal clinic in which his students try traffic and minor criminal
cases under the state student practice rule.

Made in the USA
Columbia, SC
29 December 2020